Abbey Road Studios

THE BEST STUDIO IN THE WORLD

Alistair Lawrence

Foreword by Sir George Martin

ABBEY ROAD

THE BEST STUDIO IN THE WORLD

BLOOMSBURY

LONDON · OXFORD · NEW YORK · NEW DELHI · SYDNEY

This edition published in 2016

Bloomsbury Publishing
London, Oxford, New Delhi, New York, Sydney

50 Bedford Square, London W1CB 3DP
www.bloomsbury.com

Art Director: Jill Plank
Editors: Monica Byles, Annabel Blackledge
Picture researcher: Josine Meijer
Cover Design: Greg Heinemann
Production Controller: Marina Asenjo

ISBN: 978-1-4088-8420-1

10 9 8 7 6 5 4 3 2 1

Pre-press production by Dexter -Premedia Ltd
Print and bound in China by C&C

Opposite:

*Director of Engineering, Peter Cobbin, photographed
some of the Abbey Road team celebrating the Grade II
listing of the pedestrian crossing outside the Studios
on 22 December 2010*

*All papers used by Bloomsbury Publishing are natural,
recyclable products made from wood grown in
well-managed forests. The manufacturing processes
conform to the environmental regulations of the
country of origin*

Contents

Recording R

Foreword

One of God's greatest gifts to the human race was Music. So much so that it is quite impossible to contemplate a world without it. But it was Man who found a way of preserving it, freezing it for later consumption so to speak. The invention of recording over a century ago has given us a fantastic store of music at our fingertips, and Abbey Road Studios led the way in this arcane art to become the hallowed centre of the world of the gramophone record.

Just fifteen years after the studios were built I walked up the steps for the first time to see Oscar Preuss, the head of Parlophone records. I had absolutely no idea what the business was about but I knew a job, however temporary, was in the offing. It was 1950 and I was broke, like most students found themselves on leaving music college, so I was grateful to accept his offer to join him as his assistant in the studios. I did not expect to be there for long but it was a welcome break for me to earn a little money for a change. I knew nothing about what was in store for me and of course I could not possibly contemplate the enormous impact it would have on my life.

The outside of Number Three Abbey Road gave no clues about its interior any more than it does to this day. The mysterious world of recording was well hidden from public view. My boss Oscar had an impressive office at the front with a window on the right of the entrance which you can see today. It is now a rather grand entrance hall. The other producers and Label chiefs had similar offices on the other side. A few yards down the corridor was Studio Three, the smallest room, which was used mainly for solo work and small ensembles, and down a couple flights of stairs you would find Studio Two, where I spent a good deal of my life with a wide range of artistes from Peter Sellers and Spike Milligan to The Beatles. The big studio, Number One, was like a vast cavern with an awe-inspiring acoustic. The Compton Organ was still in place then on the right-hand wall. The magic of the place was immediate. To say there was a buzz would be to underestimate the atmosphere. The greatest of stars would be there rubbing shoulders with each other in the canteen, Sir Malcolm Sargent and Humphrey Lyttelton, Sir Thomas Beecham in Studio One while Joe Loss and his band would be playing away in Number Two.

The producers, recording engineers, and all the unsung heroes who nursed and repaired the ever-sophisticated technology at Abbey Road combined to make it a veritable wonderland. This then is the story of the greatest studio in the world – it was my nursery along with so many brilliant stars who created their work there. It is a terrific story, well told, and even though I know most of it, I still find it captivating. So, imagine you are coming with me up those steps to the doors of Number Three Abbey Road. You will have a super time, I promise you.

Sir George Martin

May 2012

Before Abbey Road

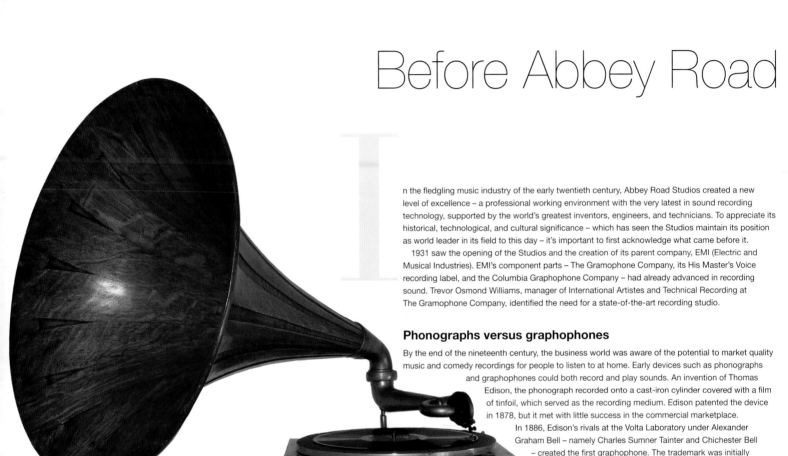

In the fledgling music industry of the early twentieth century, Abbey Road Studios created a new level of excellence – a professional working environment with the very latest in sound recording technology, supported by the world's greatest inventors, engineers, and technicians. To appreciate its historical, technological, and cultural significance – which has seen the Studios maintain its position as world leader in its field to this day – it's important to first acknowledge what came before it.

1931 saw the opening of the Studios and the creation of its parent company, EMI (Electric and Musical Industries). EMI's component parts – The Gramophone Company, its His Master's Voice recording label, and the Columbia Graphophone Company – had already advanced in recording sound. Trevor Osmond Williams, manager of International Artistes and Technical Recording at The Gramophone Company, identified the need for a state-of-the-art recording studio.

Phonographs versus graphophones

By the end of the nineteenth century, the business world was aware of the potential to market quality music and comedy recordings for people to listen to at home. Early devices such as phonographs and graphophones could both record and play sounds. An invention of Thomas Edison, the phonograph recorded onto a cast-iron cylinder covered with a film of tinfoil, which served as the recording medium. Edison patented the device in 1878, but it met with little success in the commercial marketplace.

In 1886, Edison's rivals at the Volta Laboratory under Alexander Graham Bell – namely Charles Sumner Tainter and Chichester Bell – created the first graphophone. The trademark was initially owned by the Volta Graphophone Company. This merged in 1889 with the American Graphophone Company – with an offshoot under the title of the Columbia Phonograph Company, set up as a sales operation to promote Tainter and Bell's invention. Graphophones moved away from the design of Edison's phonographs, replacing metal cylinders with cardboard ones coated with wax. The lighter cylinders produced longer recordings of superior quality. The Columbia Phonograph Company originally saw the device's potential as a dictation machine for use in offices. With this history and their considerable expense, graphophones also failed to establish

Above: *The HMV Monarch Senior Gramophone manufactured in 1905 by the Gramophone Company*
Right: *Fred Gaisberg (left) crossing the Atlantic en route to Great Britain in 1898*

themselves as desirable consumer goods. The inventions had stoked enough interest to attract investors, however. Merchandising rights to the phonograph and graphophone were sold to The North American Phonograph Company, the first music catalogues were printed, and coin-operated machines appeared in public spaces such as bars. The early years of the twentieth century also saw phonographs manufactured locally around the globe. The ambition of Edison and his rivals attracted the attention of influential businessmen and sound engineers, including the founding fathers of what would become The Gramophone Company.

Clockwise, from top left:
Gaisberg's studio in Maiden Lane; The Edison Gem Model A Phonograph by the National Phonograph Company of New Jersey, USA, early 1900s; The Klingsor Gramophone produced by Krefeld and Polyphon of Germany 1907; The Excelsior Pearl Phonograph by Excelsiorwerk of Cologne, early 1900s

Berliner and the gramophone

Emile Berliner was a German-born inventor who helped develop the loom, helicopter, telephone, record-player, radio, microphone, transformer, and acoustic tiles. In 1888, now living in the United States, Berliner invented the prototype for commercial sound recording with his inaugural flat disc and gramophone. The flat disc was a cheaper, more efficient format on which to sell commercial recordings, and soon overtook wax cylinders as the industry standard. The new format was relatively simple to produce, as Berliner incorporated electrotyping into the production process. A 'metal master' was produced – a negative of the record – which was coated in wax and submerged in acid to transfer the groove that would carry a stylus when placed on the gramophone.

Berliner settled on a shellac compound for the discs that could be mass-produced without falling foul of prior patents – the recordings proved louder and clearer than other formats available at the time. In 1893, Berliner made an astute move and invited the young sound engineer Fred Gaisberg, previously an employee of Thomas Edison, to work alongside him. After a long search for investors, the two men formed The United States Gramophone Company in 1895 to protect Berliner's patents. The Gramophone Company was established as its UK partner in 1897, with Deutsche Grammophon in 1898 and E. Berliner Gramophone of Canada in 1899. In 1898, Gaisberg moved to premises in Maiden Lane, London, to consolidate the UK business.

Gaisberg's contribution

As the industry's interest in recorded sound continued apace, opportunities opened up for engineers in the field. For Gaisberg, this meant his rise to prominence as the principal recording engineer in the early days of The Gramophone Company. He travelled the world with a brief to convince the classical music stars of the day to make their first recordings, and oversaw the earliest precursor to Abbey Road – setting up a makeshift recording studio in 1898, in the basement of the Maiden Lane offices.

From left: *Gaisberg (left) with composer Pietro Mascagni (centre) and a group of performers at The Gramophone Company's Milan Studios in 1915; Gaisberg and William Sinkler Darby with their mobile recording equipment in Leipzig, May 1899; An HMV advertisement for recordings by Enrico Caruso; Workers leave the Gramophone Company's factory in Hayes*

In his early years at The Gramophone Company, Gaisberg served as an 'Expert', charged with travelling the globe, finding and recording the artists whose output was then released on the company's His Master's Voice label. Records were manufactured at The Gramophone Company's factory in Hayes, Middlesex, founded in 1907 to produce wax discs and make parts for gramophones. Gaisberg and his colleague and old school friend William Sinkler Darby soon emerged as the two chief recording engineers. Their position conferred an air of prestige and adventure as they descended on different locales, working all hours to capture the most vibrant and impressive music from around the world. The unfamiliar equipment they unveiled puzzled border guards and impressed passers-by – more than once the engineers were even mistaken for magicians.

Recording artists

One challenge facing the early sound engineers still persists – convincing those they wished to work with to trust new technology. Gaisberg's proposal was so far from precedent that it was easy to understand some musicians' scepticism. Until that point their job had been to perform live, and even incentives such as lucrative recording contracts with royalty agreements failed to convince them to record their renditions.

While the gramophone had improved the quality of sound recordings, labels initially struggled to convince prominent classical artists to join their revolution. One of Gaisberg's notable early achievements came in 1902, when he recorded the famous tenor Enrico Caruso in Milan, Italy. Reputedly, on receiving the urgent cable from London: "Fee exorbitant, forbid you to record", Gaisberg nonetheless achieved his coup – guaranteeing the singer's fee out of his own pocket (although this story is disputed). This was one of the first collaborations with international artists. Italian tenor Beniamino Gigli, Australian soprano Nellie Melba, and Austrian-born violinist and composer Fritz Kreisler were soon to follow, eventually leading to Gaisberg recording full operas, such as the legendary Pietro Mascagni's *Cavalleria rusticana* in Milan in 1915.

Factory settings

In addition to his international forays, The Gramophone Company's factory in Hayes also provided Gaisberg with another forum for innovation. Having previously set up a makeshift recording studio in Maiden Lane, Hayes provided him with the surroundings to try something more bespoke. Unlike the later setting of Abbey Road Studios, however, there were no recognisable microphones – performers would sing into an acoustic horn in the wall, modulating the volume of their voice by leaning in closer or moving further away.

From left: *A Stollwerck chocolate disc gramophone 1902; The G&T Experimental Home Recording Machine, 1900; Toti dal Monte with a paper diaphragm gramophone 1924; The Columbia Experimental Moving Coil Microphone 1924; The Western Electric Condenser Microphone 1922*

The outbreak of the First World War proved the impetus for The Gramophone Company's relocation to Hayes in its entirety. Having expanded the site in 1912, the mass production of discs now allowed cost savings to pass to customers. Records became cheaper, fuelling the public's craving for quality recordings. People turned to gramophones for light relief from the rigours of wartime.

The company's fledgling recording studio provided new opportunities for popular recording artists of the day, such as the English contralto Louise Kirkby Lunn – known for her renditions of Wagner, Italian operatic baritone Mario Sammarco – sometimes accused of over-egging his acting, and Polish virtuoso pianist Ignacy Jan Paderewski – technically the first political figure to record for HMV as he was later elected second Prime Minister of the Republic of Poland. Following Gaisberg's recording of Caruso on his travels, contemporary artists soon spotted the potential of making recordings to further their career. Caruso's releases broadened HMV's catalogue beyond comic songs, band recordings, and ballads and are considered a significant factor in his rise to stardom in the early 1900s.

By the end of dinner a very cheerful spirit prevailed, and the room was cleared for Ponting and his lantern, whilst the gramophone gave forth its most lively airs.

Captain R. F. Scott, *Scott's Last Expedition,* **Volume 1**

The rise of the gramophone

Gramophones were manufactured at Hayes from 1919, with The Gramophone Company's return to commercial activity following involvement in the war effort. They sold over 60,000 gramophones and six million records in their first year of production alone. Sales had continued to grow even during the years of conflict, as people added to their record collections with domestically produced recordings. Interestingly, recordings by German artists had made up roughly half of the UK record market prior to the war years.

The Gramophone Company popularized the gramophone and record format, but it had a host of competitors. These produced gramophones ranging from affordable models to ornate pieces for customers who sought to impress. Keen to attract interest in their products and music catalogues, companies promoted merchandise through clever loans to prominent figures. The Gramophone Company donated the HMV Senior Monarch ('The Scott Gramophone') to R.F. Scott's expedition to the Antarctic in 1910. This was overshadowed by the expedition's tragic end, but evidence of the machine's use survives in the explorer's diaries. The gramophone remains in working order in the EMI Trust's museum today.

From paper fans to chocolate discs

The Klingsor Gramophone produced in Germany from 1907 boasted a set of strings in its front panel that vibrated as the sound played. It was one of the high-end devices of the day, some of which even featured dancing figures in the recess below the horn. Another eye-catching example was the HMV Model 460 Lumière, with a gold paper fan in place of the horn. Produced in Hayes, it was first displayed, to an invited audience, at the Piccadilly Hotel in London in 1924. The paper diaphragm offered improved sound quality, but was easily damaged. The Lumière series was thus removed from the HMV catalogue after just a year in production.

More trial and error is evident with the G&T Experimental Home Recording Machine. Produced in 1900, it was designed to record and play back. The model was never adopted due to lack of public interest in home recording. Meanwhile German confectioners Stollwerck seized the opportunity to bring a novelty to the market, producing a pair of small gramophones, based on American toy models, designed to accompany another innovation: chocolate discs. This confectionery came wrapped in tinfoil, presumably not with longevity in mind, although a few examples survive in the EMI Trust's museum – with the assurance that they play better than they now taste.

Moving on to microphones

Technology moved on towards the creation of devices with a closer resemblance to the modern microphone. Designs that fell by the wayside included the Columbia Experimental Moving Coil Microphone – an electromagnetic moving coil model from 1925. It failed because less than half of its wire-gauge coil lay within the magnetic field between the poles, resulting in poor efficiency.

The Western Electric Condenser Microphone, first manufactured in 1922, proved popular for recording onto both disc and film. Used by The Gramophone Company, the Columbia Graphophone Company, and EMI to make their first electrical recordings, it was eventually superseded by high-quality ribbon- and coil-type microphones.

"
Oh, to be home again, Down in old virginny, with my very best friend,

They call him ragtime willie. Would-a-been nice just t'see the folks,

Listen once again to the stale jokes, That big rockin' chair won't go nowhere.
"

Paul Robeson, *Rockin' Chair,* **His Master's Voice, 1931**

The EMI merger of March 1931 resulted in a shared home, based at Hayes, for three renowned music labels, as well as a scattering of smaller brands. His Master's Voice, owned by The Gramophone Company, remained the most prestigious. But the new enterprise also housed Columbia Records, which had started life in New York in the neighbourhood from which it took its name. A successor to the Volta Graphophone Company, it survives today as the oldest brand name in pre-recorded sound, relating to its early history producing pre-recorded discs. After it went into receivership in 1923, it was eventually acquired by its English subsidiary, the Columbia Graphophone Company, in 1925. Two years later, the Columbia Graphophone Company had also acquired Parlophone, formed in 1923 as the British branch of the German label Parlophon, which already had a reputation as a jazz stable. The merger between The Gramophone Company and the Columbia Graphophone Company now enabled all parts of the business to thrive.

Naming rights

This hat-trick of top record labels gave EMI an enviable back catalogue and paved the way for further development. As its creative heart at Abbey Road Studios – the world's first state-of-the-art, custom-built recording centre – was also due to be unveiled in North London in November 1931, it was decided that each of its three studios should bear the name of one of the established labels. HMV took Studio One, Columbia Studio Two, and Parlophone Studio Three. The stage was set for the next chapter in their histories.

Left: *A collection of record labels from the history of the music industry*
Right: *The unique purple labels reserved by HMV for its royal recordings*

How the Abbey Road technicians
converted sound waves

Abbey Road's founding fathers

into subtle soundscapes

1929 to 1939
The early years

EMI Studios – as it was then known – officially opened its doors on 12th November, 1931. Bought by The Gramophone Company for £16,500 in 1929, the nine-bedroom Georgian mansion in the heart of St. John's Wood – London's first garden suburb – had been transformed into the world's first custom-built recording studio.

Demand for a bespoke recording studio featuring the latest in recording technology had been established by Trevor Osmond Williams, manager of The Gramophone Company's International Artistes and Technical Recording departments. As with any new idea, the plans were not welcomed across the board. Objectors included Fred Gaisberg, who was among those initially sceptical about the company's change in ethos to require the artists to come to them, rather than the other way round.

The grand unveiling

Whatever doubts lingered about the Studios' viability were put to rest by the time of its inaugural performing session. Selected for the honour was Sir Edward Elgar, the pre-eminent English composer of his day, who was signed to His Master's Voice. This choice reflected both the allure of EMI's new venture and the musical genres that dominated recorded music during that era. Elgar, conducting the London Symphony Orchestra, marked the occasion with a crowd-pleasing rendition of his *Pomp and Circumstance March No. 1, Opus 39* – better known as *Land of Hope and Glory*. Also recorded was his dry instruction to the orchestra to "play this tune as though you've never heard it before". Captured on film, it remains the best-known and perhaps only sound film recording of Elgar. In the capacity audience of Studio 1 sat prominent figures such as George Bernard Shaw, demonstrating the significance of the event.

Left to right:

*Abbey Road Studios'
exterior in 1931; Its floor
plan from the same
year; Sir Edward Elgar
opens the Studios with
George Bernard Shaw
(seated bottom, right),
and Sir Landon Ronald
(seated bottom, left)
in attendance; Fred
Gaisberg, Elgar and the
young Yehudi Menuhin;
Menuhin and Elgar on
the steps of the Studios
in 1932*

"My idea is that there is music in the air, music all around us, the world is full of it and you simply take as much as you require.

Edward Elgar, *Letters of a Lifetime*

Main: *The orchestra assembles ahead of the Studios' grand opening.*
Inset: *Sir Edward Elgar*

Music creates order out of chaos: for rhythm imposes unanimity upon the divergent, melody imposes continuity upon the disjointed, and harmony imposes compatibility upon the incongruous.

Yehudi Menuhin

Elgar's legacy

Elgar's relationship with the Studios endured as he went on to make many recordings there. Among the soloists who recorded with Elgar was the prodigiously talented violinist Yehudi Menuhin, who would later enjoy a second career as a successful conductor and recorded in both capacities at the Studios.

"With the Elgar concerto, my recordings really centred on Abbey Road," Menuhin told BBC *Omnibus* in 1988. "It was the largest orchestra I'd ever played with as a soloist. It was a modern orchestra with all the paraphernalia that Beethoven would never have used, not even Brahms, and that was the great experience of that whole period. Preparing the concerto [that way] was Fred Gaisberg's suggestion. Elgar rather enjoyed it."

Menuhin had equally fond memories of his mentor. "I was amazed by this man who evoked so much love and response from the musicians without apparently bothering himself at all," he admitted. "I don't think he strained or sweated or exhorted or admonished – none of that. It all happened inside."

During this early era at Abbey Road, sessions were dominated by classical artists who recorded in blocks of three hours. Artists and conductors were acutely aware both of the cost of these sessions and of the opportunity they presented to create a permanent record of their endeavours.

Menuhin's abiding memories of this period appear dominated by the drive to present recorded music that was rich and evocative. "Recording was made with the romantic vision and quality of searching for expression and beauty of sound," he says, offering an appraisal of early recording techniques. "I think recordings have somewhat changed now in that they search for clarity and precision."

he man who made an indelible contribution to the art of sound recording was Alan Dower Blumlein. A gifted engineer and classical music lover, Blumlein was recruited in 1929 to the research department at Columbia, which subsequently became EMI's Central Research Laboratories based in Hayes, Middlesex. Blumlein was hired by Isaac Shoenberg, snared by the offer of a generous research budget to develop new technologies as part of EMI's sprawling remit of the time – which would later include television and several other important inventions, such as radar and the CAT scanner.

The first of many watermark achievements by Blumlein was to invent the moving-coil disc cutting head. This advance saved his employers money by eliminating significant royalties to the patent-holder – the Western Electric Corporation – of the previous method, which involved cutting discs with a moving iron. As a bonus, Blumlein's method also greatly improved the quality of the cut discs. Prior to joining Columbia, Blumlein had worked in the telecommunications branch of Western Electric. Once he had helped improve their technology; now he quickly surpassed it.

Blumlein's binaural breakthrough

What followed in 1931 was nothing short of a revelation. After an evening at the cinema, Blumlein found it incongruous that a character on one side of the frame should have their voice projected from a mono speaker on the other side of the screen. He was inspired to

From left: *Blumlein's second-generation binaural ribbon microphone; A portrait shot of A.D. Blumlein; Experimental binaural ribbon microphone without the crinkled ribbon, used for Blumlein's stereo tests; RM1A ribbon microphone, forerunner of EMI's later RM1B microphone of 1948; Two views of Blumlein's improved monophonic cutter, the EMI MC 4B*

Alan Blumlein:
The inventor of stereo

create binaural sound. To use its modern term, he created stereo recording. Two-channel audio had existed in the past – French mechanical engineer Clément Ader put it to limited use in the fields of telecommunications and short-distance broadcasts towards the end of the nineteenth century. Blumlein, at the vanguard of a company that could implement it, saw the possibilities of binaural sound to revolutionize the recorded music business. His earliest surviving notes on the subject bear the heading 'Improvements in and relating to Sound-transmission, Sound-recording and Sound-reproducing Systems'. Blumlein's binaural technology created a uniform sound field, rather than having playback from two spaced loudspeakers with a 'hole in the middle' effect.

Experiments using Blumlein's new technology began in 1931, when his creation was patented. The first binaural discs were also cut during that year. The two walls of the record's groove were cut at right angles in order to carry the two audio channels. It would take another quarter of a century for this to become standard for the recording industry, partly due to the reluctance of consumers to upgrade their listening devices. Shellac was also a difficult material and it wasn't until vinyl discs emerged in the 1950s that the right medium arrived.

Blumlein's station at Hayes provided a base from which more of his eventual 128 patents would blossom. After inventing a new style of cutting disc and then binaural sound, his work alongside colleague Herbert Holman in the early 1930s led to the creation of the moving-coil microphone, which was used in EMI recording studios and by the BBC at Alexandra Palace. Like many vintage microphones, this technology survives and some models are still in use to this day.

Blumlein was a constant thinker, problem solver, and inventor. Legend has it that his first foray into the field came at the age of seven, when he repaired his family's doorbell and presented his parents with an invoice for his handiwork from 'Alan Blumlein, Electrical Engineer'. During his adult life, his wife Doreen Lane reported that he would talk to himself in his sleep and often go straight to his notebooks in the morning to document new ideas. Often he would burn the notes he disregarded, but those that survive show very little correction or hesitation across the pages of diagrams and sentences sketching out possible new inventions and solutions.

Microphones and Blumlein pairs

In addition to moving-coil microphones, Blumlein also developed ribbon microphones, so-called because they incorporate a metal ribbon suspended in a magnetic field. As with Blumlein's cutting disc, certain elements of the technology had been patented, so he used a different approach. In the case of ribbon microphones, this meant avoiding the use of a crinkled ribbon to add tension. Blumlein's invention featured what later became known as a 'Blumlein pair', which crossed two microphones – each enclosing a ribbon set in a figure-eight – allowing sound to be picked up from any direction. This innovation was absent from Blumlein's binaural sound patent because at the time he did not have access to figure-eight microphones, but the patent contains the acknowledgement that

Above left to right: *A&M Type 1 Frequency Bridge used by Blumlein; H2S Airborne Radar Indicator Unit; H2S scanner*
Opposite: *Microphone invented by Blumlein*

such technology could be used. It appears that the facilities available to him were often trying to catch up with his ideas.

TV tuning, radar detection, and beyond

Perhaps the only reason Blumlein didn't contribute more to the advancement of sound recording was because he was re-assigned to television research by Isaac Shoenberg in 1933. As expected, a slew of advancements and inventions to aid this emerging technology followed. His contributions included the invention of the slot antenna in 1938, which linked back to his previous work as a sound engineer with its utilization of an omni-directional signal. He also made a significant contribution to the development of the waveform structure used in the 405-line Marconi-EMI system – the first ever 'high-definition' television service – adopted by the BBC in 1936.

In the Second World War, Blumlein and the Central Research Laboratories were called upon to help the war effort, working in conjunction with the Air Ministry Telecommunications Research Establishment. Together they refined Blumlein's final great invention: H2S – the first airborne, ground-scanning radar system, and the most effective radar system of the war. Among the equipment invented by the team were the indicator unit for H2S and the scanner itself. Both were being tested on board the Halifax V9977 flight that tragically crashed in 1942, destroying the prototype and killing Blumlein and his colleagues aboard. One Air Chief Marshal called his death "a catastrophe", while the Secretary of State for Air called it "a national disaster" and news of his death was concealed for two years to avoid giving aid and comfort to the enemy. A version of Blumlein's radar system went into production in 1943 and was deployed by forces in the air and at sea. It contributed significantly to Allied successes, and continued in use into the 1990s.

The last of Blumlein's inventions to be fully realized was the Computerised Axial Tomography (CAT) scanner. Unlike radar, EMI retained the sole rights to this invention as it was not prompted by the intervention of a government body. In a familiar pattern, Blumlein and Shoenberg's invention was not put into common use until many years after its conception. Godfrey Hounsfield, a senior technician at the Central Research Laboratory, sought to bring the idea to the forefront of the department's developmental strategy but, when EMI rejected an American franchise deal, competitors lobbied Washington to introduce trade barriers allowing them to freeze out foreign competition. The genius of the invention is not in doubt, however, and a slice of EMI's legacy survives in an invention still used today.

Sir Thomas Beecham

Left to right: *An informal shot of Sir Thomas Beecham with orchestra; conducting*

Originally a Columbia recording artist, Sir Thomas Beecham was a conductor and impresario, who also founded the London Philharmonic Orchestra in 1932 and the Royal Philharmonic Orchestra in 1946. Mercurial and demanding, Beecham was nonetheless loved for his wit and humour, and achieved keynote recordings of many works. He is still held in high regard by musicians and the public more than fifty years after his death in 1961. At Abbey Road, Beecham quickly saw the benefits of Blumlein's new stereo technology and encouraged the engineer in 1934 to record the London Philharmonic's rehearsal of Mozart's **Jupiter Symphony** using his experimental cutting equipment.

After visiting Beecham in 1960 and observing his poor health, fellow conductor Sir Malcolm Sargent remarked that Beecham would never conduct at Abbey Road again. Upon learning of this, Beecham expressed a desire to hear live music and was taken to Abbey Road to attend a recording session of Rachmaninov's **Second Piano Concerto** by the Royal Philharmonic. Quoted by John Lucas in his book **Thomas Beecham: An Obsession with Music**, producer Victor Olof remembered: "He spoke through the microphone to the orchestra from the machine room… he stayed in the studio… for one take and then left, his visit lasting about 25 minutes."

" Great music is that which penetrates the ear with facility and leaves the memory with difficulty. Magical music never leaves the memory. "

Sir Thomas Beecham

Beecham didn't just use the Studios to record. He also made use of the space to audition members for his own orchestra in the early 1930s. He funded that venture and many of his recording sessions from the healthy income he received as a result of his output for the Columbia catalogue which would provide them with many of their flagship releases.

Beecham the autocrat

Beecham's career also marks a long working partnership with the producer Walter Legge. Passionate about classical music, Legge was first employed at HMV from 1927 to write liner notes for record sleeves and copy for the company's retailing magazine. A protégé of Fred Gaisberg, Legge met Beecham in 1934 and at the latter's insistence was brought in as producer on his sessions. Their collaboration arose in part because Beecham and Gaisberg did not get along – but in truth, the conductor was impressed with Legge's flair and breadth of musical knowledge. For an artist so important to Columbia as Beecham, he had great leverage when making demands – indeed, he was one of a small handful of classical artists whose sales remained strong in the pop explosion of the 1950s, although by that time he had moved to HMV.

The standing of Beecham within EMI's roster also allowed him some leeway in regard to his behaviour during recording sessions. This included routinely arriving late and changing his mind as to what he was going to record at the beginning of a session. His habit in later years of recording different parts from different works in succession also made life difficult for the balance engineers, once tape recording had become the norm at the start of the 1950s. Because of his reputed good humour throughout, it's impossible to find a record of anyone bearing a grudge against him for it.

Another reason Beecham was well-liked within the classical community was his backing of contemporary classical artists whose work he admired. In particular, Beecham was instrumental in bringing the work of composer Frederick Delius to a wider audience. A British composer, Delius began composing in 1884 when he turned his back on a job managing an orange plantation in Florida and adopted African-American music as an unusual influence. Beecham is also responsible for what are considered to be the definitive recordings of Finnish composer Jean Sibelius. As with another of Beecham's favourites, Beethoven, Sibelius worked on a series of symphonies, each of which carried on from the next to form a complete, vast body of work. Beecham made several landmark recordings and in 1955 was honored by the government of Finland in for his services to Sibelius's music.

Rubinstein arrives

A classical pianist who left Germany ahead of the First World War, Arthur Rubinstein was already an international touring star before Abbey Road was founded. The Studios enabled him to immortalize his famed Chopin interpretations and further his career and by the 1940s he was firmly established as part of its catalogue. His influence his record label was felt when he expressed his displeasure at the Studios potentially recording German musicians with Nazi sympathies post-World War Two, which led to its artists and repertoire department only signing artists cleared by the de-Nazification courts.

More classics, operetta, jazz, and music hall

Left to right:

Artur Schnabel; John Brownlee; Jack Hylton and his band; Jascha Heifetz and Arthur Rubinstein; Béla Bartók; Noël Coward & Caroll Gibbons; Sidney Torch; Fats Waller; Chesney Allen and Bud Flanagan

In addition to luminary composers, conductors, and virtuosos such as Elgar, Beecham, and Menuhin, EMI's classical recording stable from the early days of Abbey Road featured legendary violinist Jascha Heifetz, pianists Arthur Rubinstein and Artur Schnabel, Hungarian composer Béla Bartók, the internationally acclaimed Australian baritone John Brownlee, and light composer Sidney Torch.

Both Heifetz and Rubinstein arrived at the Studios via the United States, where they had settled from Lithuania and Poland respectively, indicating how quickly the Studios had established itself with a global reputation. An Austrian Jew, Schnabel left his home in Berlin in 1933 with the rise of the Nazi Party and went on to record at Abbey Road over the following two decades. During this period, in addition to the five piano concertos, Schnabel recorded the first complete set of all 32 Beethoven piano sonatas at the Studios. Taking more than ten painstaking years to record on some 100 discs, these became regarded as the definitive set of recordings, leading US critic and journalist Harold C. Schonberg to dub him "the man who invented Beethoven".

Collaborations such as that between British raconteur Noël Coward and American-born bandleader Carroll Gibbons were also given a home to record together. Gibbons' rise to co-leader of the New Mayfair Orchestra further established him as part of the HMV cohort. Seminal US jazz pianist Fats Waller made several recordings on the Studios' Compton theatre organ, breathing new life into it – apparently helped by tots of whisky between takes. The album **Fats Waller in London** collects his recordings from 1938 to 1939 on the organ and piano, and includes his six-part **London Suite.** Another jazz star to record there was the British bandleader and impresario Jack Hylton, whose new style of jazz was influenced by American dance music of the day.

Music hall double act Bud Flanagan and Chesney Allen also starred. Their most popular song **Underneath the Arches** was recorded in 1931, and their stock rose through the war years, where their gentle humour understandably helped boost morale.

Classical and popular stars

Left to right: *Feodor Chaliapin; Alfred Cortot; Peter Dawson; Eileen Joyce; Emanuel Feuermann; Beniamino Gigli; Edwin Fischer; Fritz Kreisler; Adolf Busch with Reginald Kell and his quartet*

Many stars of the classical world recorded at Abbey Road during the 1930s. Feodor Chaliapin, a self-taught Russian opera singer with a bass voice who recorded for His Master's Voice and helped popularize Russian operas in the West. Swiss pianist and conductor Alfred Cortot also recorded at the Studios in the 1930s, but his support of the German occupation of France from 1941 curtailed his career and thereafter he was declared persona non grata. Australian bass-baritone Peter Dawson had great success during his career with EMI. Signed to HMV from 1904, he continued to record, often at Abbey Road, until 1958. His flexible vocal style allowed him to sing both complex classical pieces – as well as popular Scottish airs under the pseudonym Hector Grant, for EMI's Zonophone record label. By the start of the Second World War, Dawson had sold an astonishing 12 million albums.

Australian pianist Eileen Joyce made her first recording at Abbey Road in 1933. Celebrated for her Tchaikovsky and Rachmaninoff concertos, at her peak she was as popular as Gracie Fields and Vera Lynn. Ukrainian cellist Emanuel Feuermann was a musician of Jewish descent, forced to relocate from Berlin in the early 1930s because of the rise of the Nazis. Along with many other refugee musicians, he was welcomed into London's cultural scene and found his place as one of Thomas Beecham's favoured soloists.

A notable addition to EMI's canon of opera stars was the Italian tenor Beniamino Gigli. Considered a successor to Enrico Caruso after the latter's death in 1921, Gigli's own extensive career drew to a close with his final recordings of songs at Abbey Road in the early 1950s. Classical pianist and conductor Edwin Fischer was another Swiss national, whose repertoire of J.S. Bach, Mozart, Beethoven, and Schubert earned him plaudits. His recordings included the first complete traversal of Bach's **The Well-Tempered Clavier** for EMI. Taking three years to record because of other commitments, it was finally completed in 1936.

The great classicists

Austrian-born violinist and composer Fritz Kreisler's star had risen by the time he premiered Elgar's ***Violin Concerto*** – a work commissioned by and dedicated to him – in 1910. He recorded at Abbey Road during the 1930s, before he was displaced by the Second World War to the United States. His preference during recordings was to wear carpet slippers to avoid any hint of 'sliding soles'. He would also measure the humidity of the chamber before selecting his violin for the piece, tossing the alternative instrument casually into a corner.

One Anglo-German relationship not hindered by the war was that between German violinist and composer Adolf Busch and English clarinettist Reginald Kell. Busch opposed Nazism from its outset and relocated to the USA via a brief spell in Switzerland. Kell, a noted soloist of the chamber music scene, recorded at the Studios alongside Busch and the London Philharmonic and Royal Philharmonic orchestras – and in his own right as a solo artist. Other big names of the day included English conductor Sir Henry Wood. He led the London Proms for almost 50 years – bringing live classics and popular music to the people. From Spain came classical guitarist Andrés Segovia and Catalan cellist and conductor Pablo Casals. Casals collaborated with Alfred Cortot until 1937 and spent his last years in exile from Franco's regime in France.

One famous artist who did not like Abbey Road was Arturo Toscanini, the pre-eminent, perfectionist Italian conductor, who worked with Enrico Caruso and Feodor Chaliapin, among others. EMI set up a recording session for him at Abbey Road but he disliked the sound so much that he walked out. For one of the world's most famous conductors to exit without recording a note because the sound of the studio was so unacceptable to him was a complaint that had to be taken seriously. Studio 1 was later completely overhauled acoustically to provide a bigger and more natural acoustic concert-hall type of sound, which it still provides today.

Paul Robeson at Abbey Road

Recording artist, actor, athlete, scholar, and civil rights advocate, Paul Robeson first visited Abbey Road Studios in 1931, although his recording career with EMI predates that. From 1928 to 1939, the American singer was based in London, recording 170 songs. It was the first of two spells at the Studios, separated by the Second World War and Robeson's blacklisting as a result of his vocal support of Communism, the result of a personal awakening to racial politics. In 1950 Robeson was denied a passport and in 1956 was called before the US House Un-American Activities Committee to confirm whether or not he was a member of the Communist Party. Robeson refused to answer many of the Committee's questions. When his passport was finally reinstated in 1958 Robeson's travels included a return to London and Abbey Road Studios.

A modern celebrity

Robeson began his recording career with RCA in the USA but moved to HMV in the UK after his breakout performance in Show Boat at Drury Lane in 1928, helped by a classic rendition of *Ol' Man River*. Many of the tracks he recorded came from the films he starred in during the 1930s, as Robeson proved an early example of the cross-pollination between recorded music and onscreen performances that later played a key role in Abbey Road's recorded output. In total, Robeson sold over a million records – a huge figure at the time. His earliest recording at Abbey Road was a collaboration with the Englishman Ray Noble. With Noble, another diversely skilled character who counted bandleader, composer, arranger, radio comedian, and actor among his performing credits, he recorded *Rockin' Chair*, a track by legendary American composer Hoagy Carmichael. Several of Carmichael's standards – *Stardust, Georgia on My Mind*, and *Heart and Soul* – contributed significantly to the genus of pop music and were an early indicator of how a popular star of record, stage, and screen such as Robeson broadened its remit. *Rockin' Chair* was recorded on 17th September 1931 and was the first published recording made inside the Studios, as it predates Elgar's official opening performance by two months.

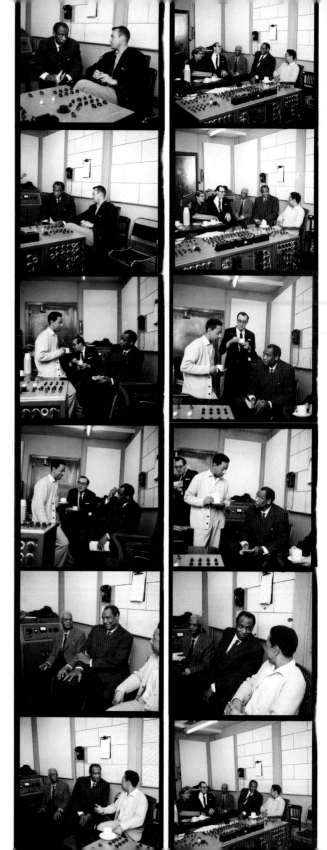

Engineers and technicians

Recording artists and producers may have occupied the limelight at Abbey Road, but its myriad engineers and technicians were vital to its success. The latter were nicknamed 'The Amp Room' – a reference to one type of equipment they were charged with transporting, maintaining, and setting up around the Studios, and a soubriquet that survives to this day. A strong dress code prevailed with porters wearing brown coats, technicians and engineers white ones, and all employees charged with wearing a collar and tie at all times. The then prime minister Winston Churchill famously remarked upon his visit to the Studios that it "looked like a hospital" because of the men in white coats.

Working your way up

Left: *Edward 'Chick' Fowler working on a wax recording during his time as an engineer in the 1930s. Before working in Hayes he was the first resident engineer in EMI's Milan office, where he made all manner of recordings, from opera to speeches by Mussolini.*

An example of an engineer from the early days, visibly promoted through the ranks at Abbey Road, was Edward 'Chick' Fowler – who eventually managed the Studios. An engineer throughout the 1930s, Fowler and his colleagues worked on the first mixing desks, which preceded multi-track recording, and were tasked with engineering whatever genre of music or recording artist came through the door. At times the job was certainly laborious. In the days before magnetic tape recordings were captured on wax and, during one session with famed but volatile Austrian pianist Artur Schnabel, Fowler used 29 sheets of wax to capture one particular side as the waxes could not be re-used like tape or a digital track.

Fowler experienced both the zenith of classical recording and the rise of pop music. Over 30 years of service, he dealt with everything from the niceties of achieving the best recording from an artist to managing the building's security in the era of The Beatles.

The royal microphones

Occasionally, sound engineers move away from invention and recording long enough to create a prestige item. The first of the 'royal microphones' – one was made for each monarch – was manufactured by the French company Marconi for George V in 1925. A carbon microphone placed inside a hollowed-out block of marble, it was used to record the king when he spoke to the nation. Fred Gaisberg had spotted the opportunity on his travels, and instigated the acquisition of Marconi by The Gramophone Company in 1929. With the business came the royal commission. Microphones for King George VI and H.M. Queen Elizabeth (later the Queen Mother) were made c.1937 and used the more familiar moving-coil principle.

Recording *The King's Speech*

The award-winning 2010 movie **The King's Speech** covered the challenges faced by King George VI and his speech therapist in overcoming a nervous stammer to broadcast live to the nation – specifically his keynote address concerning Britain's declaration of war on Germany on 3 September 1939. Technology of the time did not allow for the speech to be pre-recorded and the King's words were transmitted live down a telephone wire to Abbey Road Studios, where they were recorded onto disc for posterity.

Rediscovered by Peter Cobbin, Director of Engineering at the Studios, the five existing royal microphones were brought out of storage when director Tom Hooper and composer Alexandre Desplat approached Abbey Road about recording the soundtrack for the film. The three earliest microphones were restored to working order by Lester Smith in time for composer and conductor Desplat to record the orchestra through them, in conjunction with other microphones. The film's opening score is a recording solely from the three vintage mics. Actor Colin Firth's recorded speeches were played out through Studio 1 and recaptured via the royal microphones, faithfully recreating the sound and tone of George VI's original, famous wartime speeches.

" It is to this high purpose that I now summon my people at home and my peoples across the seas, who will make our cause their own. I ask them to stand calm, firm and united in this time of trial "

King George VI, address to the nation at the outbreak of the Second World War

How the Second World War
affected the music industry

The war and its aftermath

and created iconic recording stars

The 1940s
Wartime and beyond

Predictably, the seismic shift caused by the Second World War caused a downturn in the output of EMI's recording labels. The range of artists who could record at Abbey Road Studios was reduced as international travel became difficult. In particular, hubs of classical music such as Berlin, Vienna, and Milan could no longer support artists from Britain or the United States, and many musicians were enlisted to fight, or were trapped on opposing sides of the divide.

Enlistment was not an insurmountable barrier for making music, though. The gramophone market remained robust as people turned to recordings to keep up their spirits. As a result, many artists became almost iconic – with some recording in uniform in a bid to help the war effort and boost morale. Two such individuals were the prodigious British horn player Dennis Brain and his compatriot the pianist Denis Matthews, who both recorded at Abbey Road during breaks in national service. Brain's solo career began in earnest in 1943, when he shot to fame after his performance of Benjamin Britten's **Serenade for Tenor,** **Horn and Strings**, which had been written partly for him. Matthews made his professional debut in 1939, and remained enlisted until 1946. Both artists survived the war.

An embattled soundtrack

Fortunately, shellac (the material used for manufacturing discs) remained unrationed in the UK during this period, although in the US record production was reduced by 75 per cent. Aware, however, of its clientele's beleaguered income, EMI restricted the number of its releases during the war years and promoted budget-priced catalogues such as Columbia's DX dark blue label and HMV's C Series plum label. Funded by the British Council to promote British culture overseas, the C Series highlighted uniquely British composers such as John Gay and William Walton, and was also popular at home.

EMI's strategy judged the public mood well and ensured the company's survival until it could rebuild operations at the end of the war.

Main: *Dennis Brain, dubbed a prodigy by Thomas Beecham, performs at Abbey Road Studios*

Inset: *Brain records with Denis Matthews in Studio 3. Matthews, like Brain, served with the RAF during the war before continuing a successful career as a concert pianist.*

> Next to a letter from home, Captain Miller, your organization is the greatest morale builder in the European Theater of Operations.

General James Doolittle, United States Army Air Forces

From left: *Glenn Miller and Dinah Shore recording together at Abbey Road Studios; Miller with his orchestra in 1944; A portrait shot of Miller in uniform*

Perhaps the greatest wartime star to record at Abbey Road was Glenn Miller. In 1942, aged 38 and drawing huge audiences as a trombonist and swing bandleader, he was nonetheless turned down by the US Navy as too old to be drafted. The military eventually signed him up as part of their drive to maintain troop morale by offering the best in entertainment. Miller swiftly set about modernizing the band of the Army and Air Force. Acutely aware of his music's commercial appeal, Miller prided himself on delivering note-perfect performances to please the masses. His tunes became the quintessential wartime soundtrack for millions – not least because of their ubiquity on radio and the big screen, as well as on records, which flew off the shelves. The presence of American servicemen in Britain during the war years – as well as the influence of top bandleaders – changed the face of popular music in a generation.

Miller's final session

The legendary visit of Glenn Miller and his Army Air Force Orchestra to Abbey Road on 16 September, 1944, was tragically the last time he recorded. Shortly afterwards, a plane carrying Miller and his band en route to salute troops in Paris disappeared in bad weather over the English Channel leaving no survivors. A collaboration with popular actor and TV entertainer Dinah Shore, the recording was not heard until 50 years later when its European copyright expired. It survives today, however, alongside the Glenn Miller Orchestra – which reformed in 1953.

Right: *A trio of shots showing Gracie Fields visiting Abbey Road Studios*
Opposite: *(main) George Formby recorded at Abbey Road throughout the war years. He was one of the first entertainers to visit Normandy after the invasion. (inset top) Al Bowlly and Jimmy Mesene record at the Studios, 1941; (inset bottom) Kathleen Ferrier and Gerald Moore*

As the nation pulled together in support of the war effort, many artists who were not enlisted served their country by touring to entertain the troops, and pluckily braving the Blitz to record at home. At Abbey Road, approximately a third of the engineering workforce was reassigned either to radio work or to hush-hush government work commissioned at EMI's factory in Hayes.

The Entertainments National Service Association (ENSA) had a considerable impact on the Studios' output. Formed in 1939, ENSA brought entertainment to British armed forces personnel and munitions workers for the duration of the war. It operated within the Army, Navy, and Air Force and owned many recordings made during the period; it was the original owner of Glenn Miller's session at Abbey Road. ENSA recordings were produced as discs and released to military units, but were not available to the general public. Artists were still entitled to record for commercial release, but their availability, as well as that of studios and technicians, was reduced in the battle to keep the forces cheerful in the face of Hitler. By the end of the war in 1945, over 80 per cent of all British entertainers had signed up to ENSA.

Fighting spirit

As an epicentre for recording, Abbey Road nonetheless continued to attract favourite performers of the era. Among the best-loved was home-grown film and music hall star Gracie Fields, who empathized greatly with the hardships of wartime because of her working-class childhood. Fields signed up to ENSA and toured widely to entertain the troops, although her marriage to Italian-born film director Monty Banks in 1940 subsequently made it difficult for her to stay in Britain. Despite her relocation to California, so that her husband could avoid internment, Fields returned regularly to the UK to record at Abbey Road Studios and perform to troops and factory workers.

Dubbed the Forces' Sweetheart, Vera Lynn similarly carried the flag for fighting corps and the families they left behind, giving numerous outdoor concerts to servicemen in Egypt and India, even to guerrilla units in occupied Burma. Signed to Decca, she did not record at Abbey Road until 1962, when she released her album **Hits from the Blitz** for HMV during her fifteen-year stay with EMI. In 2009, Decca issued her album of digitally remastered top hits, which shot to No. 1 in the British album chart – at 92, Lynn became the oldest person to achieve this honour.

Contralto Kathleen Ferrier was initially self-taught, and had worked for the General Post Office. In wartime, she gave concerts across Britain under the auspices of CEMA (the Council for the Encouragement of Music and the Arts). In 1942, Ferrier was spotted by renowned conductor Sir Malcolm Sargent: impressed with her skill and classical repertoire, he helped her steep rise to fame. Ferrier recorded at Abbey Road in 1944, accompanied by the English pianist Gerald Moore. An 'unashamed accompanist' – it was the title of his autobiography – Moore also worked with Pablo Casals, among others.

We'll meet again, Don't know where, don't know when.

But I know we'll meet again, some sunny day.

Vera Lynn, *We'll Meet Again*

Doing their bit for the war effort

British dance bandleader Harry Roy recorded a few tracks in the Studios during the years of national emergency. The founder and leader of Harry Roy's Tiger Ragamuffins, he was notable for his residency at the Embassy Club in 1942 and later for his tour of the Middle East, where he entertained the troops.

Having left Vienna for London in 1938, Austrian tenor Richard Tauber recorded at Abbey Road Studios during the 1940s. Perhaps because of his strong antipathy towards the Nazis, and the fact that his first London performance was under Sir Thomas Beecham, Tauber rejected lucrative offers from America and stayed in Britain throughout the war. Similarly attracted to the UK for patriotic reasons was English performer Gertrude Lawrence. A star of Broadway and West End theatre, she eagerly signed up to ENSA. It took some time to clear the paperwork – Lawrence was married to an American and based in Dennis, Massachusetts – but she eventually succeeded. She performed hours after touchdown from her 36-hour flight from Washington to a mix of British and American servicemen. The soldiers who attended her concert, among them her husband, were awaiting deployment on the imminent D-Day invasion of Normandy. Lawrence eventually followed as part of an ENSA unit that also included Ivor Novello, performing wherever they could find a suitable public space.

Solomon puts his foot in it

A special mention should perhaps be reserved for British classical pianist Solomon. A child prodigy, Solomon recorded for his entire career at the Studios and also performed recitals in the USA and Australia during the war. He is remembered for storming out of Abbey Road during one recording session, dismayed that a dog someone had let roam the studio had fouled his piano pedals – something he didn't discover until it was too late.

Left to right: *Solomon plays the piano at the Studios without incident; Band leader Harry Roy; Austrian singer Richard Tauber; 'Lassie from Lancashire' Gertrude Lawrence*

After weeks of more or less patient waiting, repeated timid, pleading, urgent, and finally importunate requests to the authorities who rule such matters in Washington and London, and a rapid-fire barrage of telegrams, cables, and telephone calls, it had happened. At last I had permission to do what I had been wanting desperately to do for four years – go to England and do my bit on a tour for ENSA.

Gertrude Lawrence, from her memoir *A Star Danced*, 1945

This page: *Joe Loss dances, conducts, and holds court in the Studios*
Opposite: *A studio portrait of Kirsten Flagstad, inset; Kirsten Flagstad records at Abbey Road in 1948*

Joe Loss at Abbey Road

The success of big bands in the 1940s was not limited to American artists. Joe Loss, born in London's East End, was signed to EMI's budget Zonophone label in 1934 to record with his band, but his career didn't truly blossom until the 1940s. His rising star then called him to performances in royal palaces and in innumerable concert halls. The Joe Loss Orchestra was also one of the few big bands that rose to fame during the war years but managed to survive the cull caused by the explosion of pop music in the 1950s. Another high watermark in his 60-year career was a stint on the BBC's inaugural run of **Come Dancing** in 1964. His band survives to this day under the leadership of Todd Miller – an unbroken run of more than 80 years since 1930.

Casualty of war

By contrast, one artist whose career suffered greatly as a result of the war was the Norwegian soprano Kirsten Flagstad. After successfully making the transition from operettas to weightier operatic roles during the 1930s, her profile rose when her performance in Wagner's **Die Walküre** caused a stir at the Metropolitan Opera in New York City. She stayed at the Met until 1941, completing over 100 performances.

Flagstad's subsequent decision, however, to return home to Nazi-occupied Norway to reunite with her husband damaged her career. Fans in North America were offended by what was viewed as her defection. When her husband was charged with profiteering during the occupation, matters worsened. It later transpired there had been no collaboration between her family and the Nazis, but Flagstad faced a rough road back. Luckily her talent won the day. She was once more invited to perform at top venues, and to record at Abbey Road.

Introducing vinyl

After wax cylinders were rendered obsolete by the gramophone, shellac-based discs succeeded them. Different record companies used slightly different formulas for the compound on which they pressed their records, but most included mineral filler derived from rocks and cotton fibres. As a result, the compound had tensile strength, but was still quite brittle.

Surface noise was a problem that reduced over time, as the compounds became more refined. The result of this was that shellac discs continued to be manufactured into the 1950s alongside flexible, celluloid discs, although both had been replaced by vinyl as the market leader twenty years earlier.

Vinyl replaces shellac

American label and electrical goods manufacturer RCA Victor debuted their first vinyl-based compound in 1931. It was a lighter material than shellac, with less surface noise and more durability. Its only drawbacks were that it was relatively expensive and damaged by heavy, old-style gramophone needles. However, its superior quality meant that players were soon adapted to accommodate it.

Opposite: *A piece of vinyl issued by the His Master's Voice label*
Insets: *A selection of early catalogues issued by HMV*

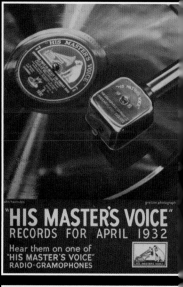

Gravity cutting motor

Left and below:

*A gravity cutting lathe
from the EMI archive,
used to cut old-style
78rpm discs*

The vinyl playback speed of 78 revolutions per minute (rpm) was adopted as the industry standard from the mid-1920s. The standards then changed after the Second World War, when Columbia marketed a 33rpm disc from 1948. In response, RCA Victor created the 45rpm format a year later. Columbia's model became the standard format for albums and RCA's the preferred model for seven-inch discs used for singles.

However, 78s were still produced and the technology used to create them survived at Abbey Road until the early 1950s. Gravity fed lathes were preferred to electrical models because they were reliable when electric supplies were not, such as during the war.

As much as the format of the discs has changed, the way they are cut has not. "It's a technology that hasn't changed in essence since they first sang into a horn and scratched it on a wax cylinder," says Sean Magee, a mastering engineer at Abbey Road. "It's changed from acoustic to electrical, but you still have a needle stuck in a groove that vibrates, which in turn moves air and you hear music. It's that simple, really."

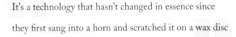

It's a technology that hasn't changed in essence since they first sang into a horn and scratched it on a wax disc

Sean Magee, mastering engineer

Cutting the groove

Abbey Road is home to one of the estimated fifty cutting lathes in the UK, a total that is thought to exceed the number in the rest of the world combined. Demand for vinyl has now diminished to the point where the lathes are no longer manufactured.

"It only gets a bit tricky if the head blows up, but I've only known that happen twice in seventeen years," says Magee. "As far as I know there's only one guy on the planet with the tools to fix one properly."

The lathes can cut grooves onto a variety of surfaces, which include a 'metal master'. The stainless steel disc covered in a copper alloy results in fewer stages in the overall processing.

"Your record will be four generations away from the 'father'," explains Magee. "From the father they grow the mother and from the mother they grow the stampers, which become the children. Collections of stampers and mothers and fathers are known as family, which is quite quaint."

Opposite: *A recording cut onto a stainless steel master disc*
Below, left to right: *Sean Magee cuts a piece of vinyl*

It only gets a bit tricky if the head blows up, but I've only known that happen twice in seventeen years...

Sean Magee, mastering engineer

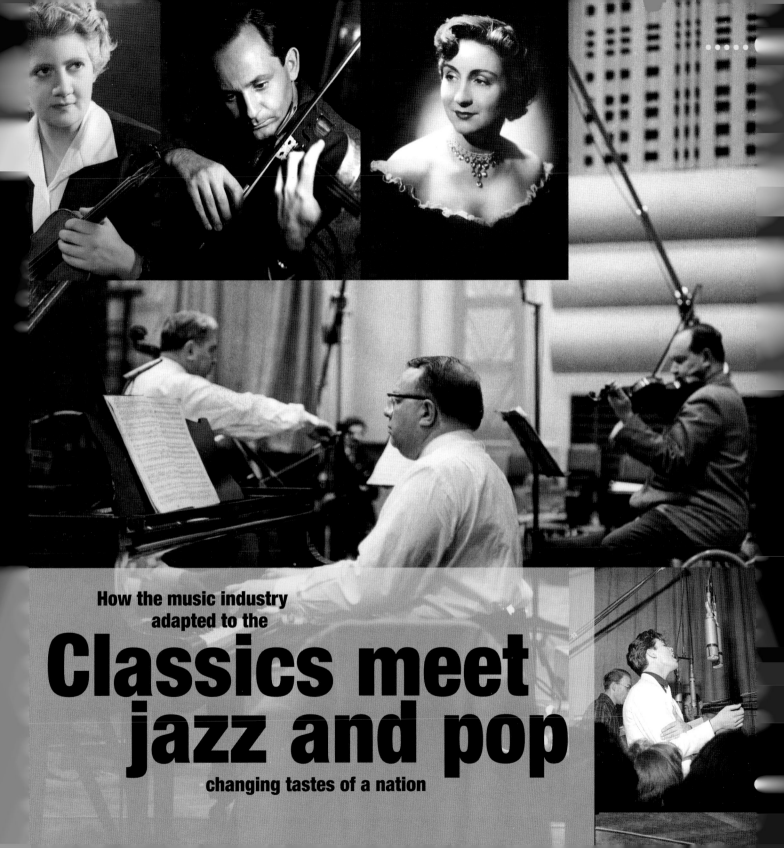

How the music industry
adapted to the

Classics meet jazz and pop

changing tastes of a nation

The 1950s
A decade of change

By the end of the 1940s, Britain was beginning to pull itself out of its postwar slump and respond to a rapidly changing musical landscape. Until that point, EMI had served largely as a conduit for transatlantic releases with the majority of pop music recordings imported from the United States. Now, however, the company looked to modernize its catalogue with more local talent.

All change at Abbey Road

Four men with musical backgrounds – Walter J. Ridley, Norman Newell, Norrie Paramor, and George Martin – were hired to work in the Studios as artist and repertoire (A&R) managers and producers. Ridley worked on the HMV label, Paramor for Columbia, and Martin for Parlophone, while Newell worked across all the labels.

This radical shift also saw an injection of new blood among the engineers. Stuart Eltham and Peter Bown were among those taken on to pioneer new methods of recording pop music, which required different techniques to those used with classical recordings. Some of the old guard struggled to adapt. When the two top-selling American pop labels – CBS and RCA Victor – split from EMI in 1952 and 1956 respectively, pressure grew for Abbey Road to start creating hits.

An early success for the new setup arrived in 1952. Max Bygraves – recruited from the successful BBC morning radio show *Educating Archie*, where he played the part of an odd-job man – kick-started his solo singing career with the novelty tune *Cowpuncher's Cantata*. It was the first Abbey Road hit to enter the charts, placed at No. 11 on the very first British Top Twelve pop chart, published by *New Musical Express* magazine on 14 November 1952. As Bygraves balanced his career across film, television, and radio his success demonstrated how EMI, sensitive to a period of transition for popular culture, once again utilized the Studios to reflect the changing tastes of a nation.

Main: *Max Bygraves*
Insets: *(top left)*
Michael Holliday with
Norrie Paramor;
(top right) Noël Coward
and Alma Cogan;
(bottom) Ruby Murray
and Frank Sinatra
in Hollywood

Brother goose, mother goose, don't you fear,

'Cos I've arrived, and to prove it, I'm 'ere.

Max Bygraves, *Cowpuncher's Cantata*

Left: *Ruby Murray recording in Studio 2*
Opposite: *An official portrait of Murray*

By 1952, the Hit Parade featured in the **New Musical Express** both reflected and shaped the career trajectory of pop artists by listing the top singles in the country, ranked by sales each week. This new arrival gave Abbey Road Studios an accurate barometer by which to measure its success during the early years of pop. Meanwhile, EMI's various labels still featured a number of artists who had become British institutions and were largely unaffected by fleeting trends. An obvious example was Noël Coward, who continued to record at the Studios as an accompaniment to his myriad stage, screen, and radio projects – which had cemented him as an idiosyncratic, international star.

Ruby Murray's record-breaking success

Seeking to up the number of female pop artists on its labels, EMI recruited Northern Irish singer Ruby Murray. Spotted at the Metropolitan Music Hall in London in 1954, she had a husky but girlish voice resulting from an operation for swollen glands at six weeks old. Having first debuted at the age of 12 on Irish television, the knock-out sex appeal of Murray's vocal delivery helped

awaken mainstream audiences to EMI's regenerated pop aspirations.

Signed to Columbia and produced by Norrie Paramor, Murray first entered the charts at No. 3 in 1954 with the single **Heartbeat**. She notched up seven chart entries in 1955 alone, which included the long-standing record of five separate chart positions in one week. As a result, she occupied an unheard-of one quarter of the Hit Parade. Unlike many of her peers, such as London-born vocalist Alma Cogan, Murray recorded original songs, which made her achievement all the more remarkable.

At last, the new structure at EMI and Abbey Road had proved itself. Among Murray's three chart entries for 18 February 1955, was **Softly Softly** – her first No. 1. By the end of 1955, her tunes had set another record: between them, they totalled 80 weeks of chart activity in one year. A popular artist, Murray released 19 solo singles over the course of her career. The last one – **Goodbye Jimmy, Goodbye** – charted at No. 10 in 1959. Murray's availability for recording was limited because of her commitment to television appearances and touring, but her enormous success demonstrates how quickly the Hit Parade came to influence the popularity of individual pop performers. Every one of Murray's hits was recorded at Abbey Road.

A native of Whitechapel, East London, Alma Cogan's rise to the top was unmatched by any British female artist of the 1950s; consequently, she also became the highest paid. Nicknamed 'The girl with the giggle in her voice' for her sparkling personality, Cogan recorded numerous frothy chart hits at the Studios over the decade. Her first No. 1, **Dreamboat**, came in 1955. In the style of the day, she covered songs that had previously been hits in the United States – sometimes bettering the success of the original.

The hit factory

Cogan was recommended to producer Walter Ridley in 1949, and signed to HMV to fill the need for female acts on a roster dominated by male talent. Ridley spent two years refining Cogan's voice and finding suitable material for her, before passing her into the capable hands of Norman Newell. She debuted with **Bell Bottom Blues** in 1954, and a star was eventually born. Cogan made numerous TV appearances in her trademark sequined dresses, reputedly never worn twice. She later became a friend of The Beatles, and died on tour aged 34, diagnosed with ovarian cancer.

Left: *Alma Cogan poses for a promotional photo shoot*
Right inset: *Cogan, Norman Newell, and Tony Osborne behind a mixing desk*
Right main: *Cogan recording at Abbey Road Studios*

Oh, my pa-pa, to me he was so wonderful

Oh, my pa-pa, to me he was so good

No one could be so gentle and so lovable

Oh, my pa-pa, he always understood

**O Mein Papa (translated lyrics),
written by Paul Burkhard, 1939**

Despite the fact that EMI gradually built up a repertoire of pop acts to infiltrate the Hit Parade, the first ever No. 1 recorded at the Studios was an instrumental track by a soloist trumpeter covering a German song from the 1930s. Eddie Calvert's individualistic rendition of *O Mein Papa* topped the charts in both the UK and the United States in 1954, proving that the spectrum of popular music in the 1950s was not a total revolution.

Triumphs and disappointment

A native of Preston, Lancashire, Calvert spent his formative years playing in brass bands. He turned professional after the Second World War and first recorded on the Melodisc label before moving to Columbia. *O Mein Papa* topped the Hit Parade for a then-record nine weeks and was followed by another No. 1 single, *Cherry Pink and Apple Blossom White*. The fact that both tracks were instrumental made it a unique achievement, as they were the first of their genre to have such measurable commercial success. In total, Calvert recorded seven singles at the Studios during the 1950s – all of which charted.

A versatile musician, Calvert also wrote for film, TV, and other recording artists. He was the first artist to have an instrumental track banned when his recording of the title melody to the 1956 film *The Man with the Golden Arm* – starring Frank Sinatra – was vetoed by the BBC because of the film's theme of drug use. Calvert's last Top Ten hit was *Mandy*, from the soundtrack to the British comedy *John and Julie*, which charted at No. 9 in 1958. The movie provided early roles for Sid James and Peter Sellers – the latter another Abbey Road recording artist.

The close-knit network of collaborators at Abbey Road became evident as producer and orchestra leader Norrie Paramor organized a collaboration EP release that featured friends and colleagues at EMI – Calvert, Ruby Murray, and 'the English Bing Crosby', Michael Holliday.

Only in the 1960s was Calvert's style of playing finally displaced by pop music. His last UK chart single, *Little Serenade*, peaked at a modest No. 28, and his career slowly wound down over the following decade. Disillusioned, Calvert emigrated to South Africa in 1968, where he continued to perform, and stayed until his death ten years later. With him went the gold disc he was awarded for UK sales of *O Mein Papa* – another Abbey Road first.

Left: *Eddie Calvert, 'the Man With The Golden Trumpet' in a studio shot by renowned photographer Angus McBean*

Anything but
the obvious

A n integral part of Abbey Road Studios' history, George Martin joined the EMI staff in 1950. Originally brought in to work with Parlophone head Oscar Preuss, he was a finely trained musician working as a freelance oboist but with high hopes of becoming a great pianist. Like Paramor, Ridley, and Newell, Martin was a seminal producer – not least because previously the artist's manager had always run recording sessions and there had been no such role. Parlophone was the smallest of EMI's three main labels and lacked His Master's Voice and Columbia's international catalogue.

Martin soon noticed that profits from pop music were being used to fund classical recordings. Gradually, he managed Parlophone's transition away from orchestral, traditional dance, baroque, and chamber music towards something more modern and commercially viable. Martin couldn't compete for the big-name pop stars signed to EMI's other labels so he experimented with comedy and jazz. His first comedy recordings, with British dramatist Peter Ustinov, were released in 1952. **Phoney Folklore** featured the irreverent song of the Russian peasant "whose tractor had betrayed him", while **Mock Mozart** featured a young Anthony Hopkins on harpsichord. Understandably, the venture was a huge success and set the tone for future anarchic collaborations.

Risky business

Following his boss's retirement in 1955, Martin was the clear candidate for promotion to artists' manager at Parlophone. This gave him the power he needed to further grow his roster at the label. Often working on little more than a hunch when signing a new act, his risky strategy continued to pay off, years before a certain quartet from Liverpool recorded their first demo at Abbey Road.

Right: *George Martin at the Studios*
Above: *Martin worked as a quantity surveyor and clerk as a young man, but music was more than just a desk job*

"Courage is often lack of insight, whereas cowardice in many cases is based on good information."

Peter Ustinov

Above: *Peter Sellers and Spike Milligan work in Abbey Road Studios with George Martin*

Right: *Sellers and Milligan record their* **Bridge on the River Wye** *comedy at the Studios in 1962*

Opposite: *The front cover of Spike Milligan's 1961 album* **Milligan Preserved**

George Martin's knack for recording comedy artists eventually led him to a fruitful partnership with two legendary British funny men: Peter Sellers and Spike Milligan. The pair had become famous through their hit BBC radio comedy series **The Goon Show**, which first aired in 1951. Both had served in the Second World War, and had honed their skills in making people laugh as part of ENSA. Coincidentally, Milligan was also a skilled jazz musician who played several instruments, while Sellers was a talented drummer.

Comic timing

Sellers and Milligan recorded collaborations as well as solo albums, all produced by George Martin. Milligan's solo records were first issued in the 1960s, but Sellers began in 1958 with his LP **The Best of Sellers**, and triumphed with a hit single in 1960, when George Martin instigated **Goodness Gracious Me** – his famous collaboration with the iconic Italian actress Sophia Loren.

Most of the songs performed by Sellers and Milligan were either parodies or comic stories set to music, which made liberal use of strange noises and sound effects – both artists were fond of recording loud bangs and other explosions. One Sellers track, **Suddenly It's Folksong** from 1958, reaches the conclusion of a pub being smashed up, after a row sparked by someone playing a bum note escalates into chaos. The comedian decided the best way to create the desired effect was to kick a chair across the studio. It hit Martin in the shins and the resulting cry of pain can be heard on the track.

Sellers' and Milligan's time at Abbey Road allowed them space for their anarchic ideas to take hold and flourish. In 1962, they decided to record a parody of the multiple award-winning 1957 war film **The Bridge on the River Kwai.** Alongside the youthful Jonathan Miller and Peter Cook, their production of **The Bridge on the River Wye** was originally intended to share the same name as the movie. The threat of legal action from the film's studio soon put a stop to that, and also led to Martin testing his skill as an engineer – he was required to edit out the 'K' every time the word 'Kwai' was uttered on the soundtrack.

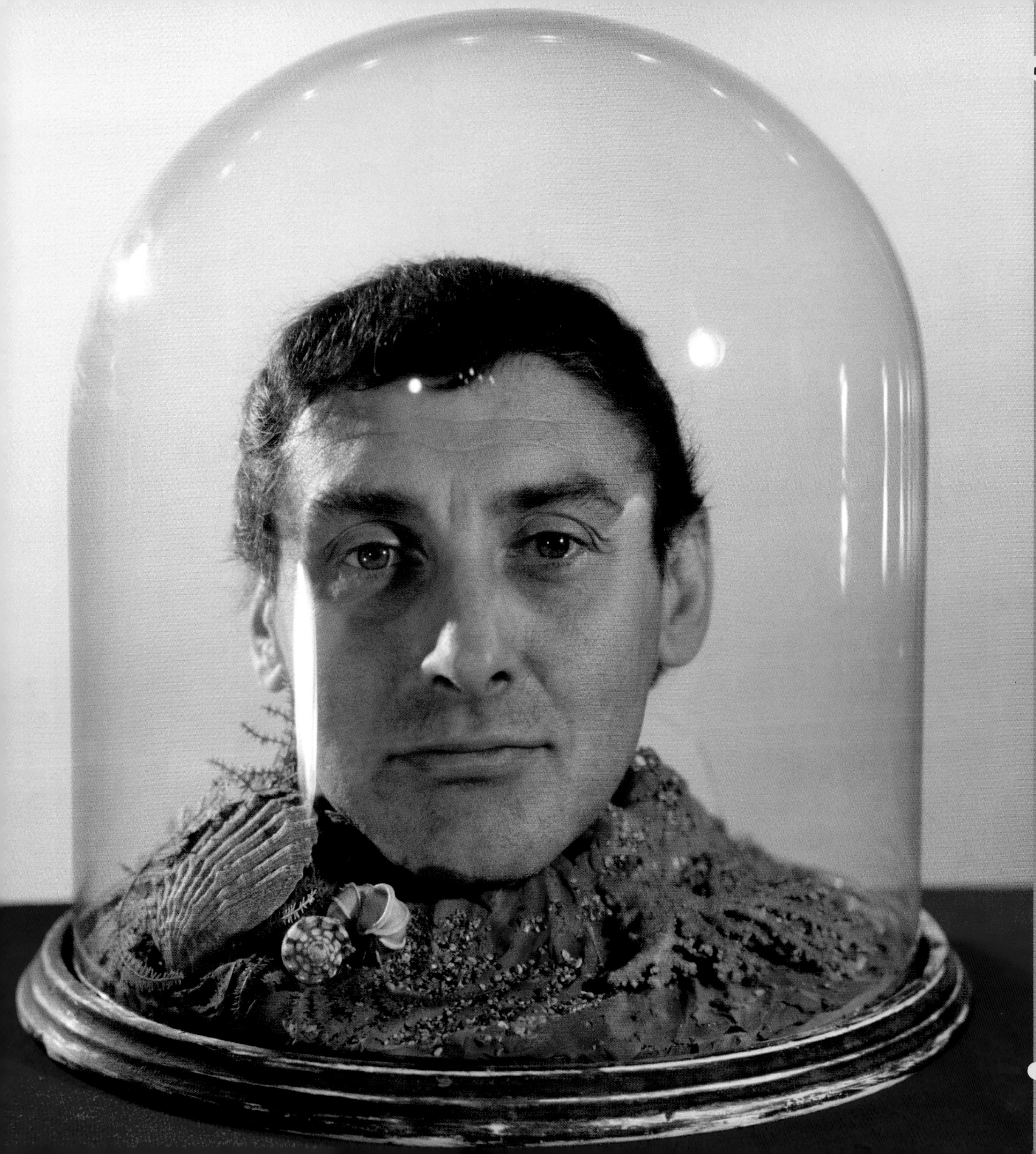

> " Mud, mud, glorious mud. Nothing quite like it for cooling the blood.
>
> So follow me follow, down to the hollow. And there let us wallow in glorious mud. "

The Hippopotamus Song, **Flanders and Swann**

From left: *Stills of Flanders & Swann recording **At the drop of a Hat**; The original disc label of **At the drop of a Hat** by Flanders and Swann; Two portrait shots of the pair*

Another comic duo to impress under Martin's stewardship at the Studios was the double act of Flanders and Swann. Old school friends who reunited to work together after the war in 1948, singer and actor Michael Flanders with pianist and composer Donald Swann first found notable success with their 1956 revue show **At the drop of a Hat**. Flanders performed from a wheelchair, having contracted polio during his wartime service in the Navy. Interspersing humorous stories with light operetta numbers, Flanders and Swann had perfected their act before they first entered a recording studio with Martin in 1957. Shrewdly, Martin decided to issue both EPs and LPs of their work.

The recorded output of Flanders and Swann included two versions of their act **At the drop of a Hat**, separated by a span of three years, during which time the piece was tweaked and refined. The second issue, in 1960, was recorded in stereo, and was their final performance. Two more albums with Martin followed: **At the drop of another Hat** in 1964 and **The Bestiary of Flanders & Swann** – a collection of animal songs from their acts not included on the earlier albums – in 1967. Most popular was **The Hippopotamus Song**, the chorus of which had been performed in the duo's live shows translated into any one of 20 languages, with two separate Latin versions.

A veritable *tour de force*

The pair performed live a great deal, to the point where the recordings that punctuated their career capably reflect the development of their art. In total, it is estimated that Flanders and Swann performed live over 2,000 times. Their first LP with Martin marked the 50th performance of **At the drop of a Hat**, to give some indication of the keen eye and quick timing with which they were signed to Parlophone.

From left: *Humphrey Lyttleton performs at his HL Club in London's Oxford Street; Assorted Lyttelton Parlophone releases*

George Martin also used his position at Parlophone to breathe new life into the British jazz scene. Largely ignored by domestic record labels, jazz was out of fashion and its artists were ripe for the picking. Trawling Soho's bars and clubs, Martin came across the charismatic trumpeter and bandleader Humphrey ('Humph') Lyttelton. Descended from aristocracy he was selected to stand at the vanguard of the jazz revolution.

Lyttelton's passion for jazz developed during his school days at Eton College during the 1930s, where his appreciation of Louis Armstrong motivated him to learn the trumpet and form a jazz quartet. A dedicated musician, there are even reports of him carrying his pistol in one hand and trumpet in the other on missions in the war years.

The Jazzman cometh

Lyttelton recorded at several London centres, but his work reverberated through pop recordings that followed. The most famous similarity is that between the distinctive piano intro to Lyttelton's **Bad Penny Blues** of 1956, recorded at IBC Studios – and **Lady Madonna** by The Beatles, recorded in 1968 at Abbey Road. The latter was a fusion of modern pop and trad jazz, sampling elements of what is now remembered as Lyttelton's most famous melody from thirteen years earlier. Both hits were released on the Parlophone label under George Martin.

Countdown to revolution

Clockwise from far right:
The sleeve from a compilation release linked to British rock and roll TV programme **Six-Five Special**; *Cliff Richard's early single* **Move It**; *Reginald Dixon's* **Blackpool Favourites**; **Songs For Swingin' Sellers** *by Peter Sellers;* **At the drop of a Hat** *by Flanders and Swann; Ray Anthony's* **Concert** *album;* **Imagination** *by The King Sisters*

As the end of the 1950s approached, the scope of recording artists at Abbey Road Studios had broadened significantly. Other artists whose discs were released by EMI in these years included Glenn Miller protégé Ray Anthony, American big band vocal quartet The King Sisters, English theatre organist Reginald Dixon, and rising UK pop star Cliff Richard – who would come to greater prominence in the following decade.

On the technical side, new engineers and producers were also changing with the times, their ideas for the future brimming with the same genius for innovation as their predecessors. Even so, no one could have predicted that another quantum leap forward in recorded music was just around the corner – or that Abbey Road Studios was about to become a truly global force.

SIX-FIVE SPECIAL !

(Based on the successful B.B.C. T.V. Series)

Recorded with many of its original Artists

JOHN BARRY SEVEN   JIM DALE
JIMMY JACKSON   KING BROTHERS
KEN JONES   DON LANG
LAURIE LONDON   GEOFF LOVE
TONY OSBORNE   TERRY WAYNE
and THE RITA WILLIAMS SINGERS

PARLOPHONE
LONG PLAYING 33⅓ R.P.M. RECORD

Photo: DAILY HERALD

**How rock and roll
and technical wizardry**

The sounds
of the 60s

took the world by storm

The 1960s
Science of sound

From its creation, Abbey Road Studios served as a top-level experimental laboratory in the field of sound registration, and the 'men in white coats' – the technical engineers – carried its scientific credentials.

The white coats, that for many years distinguished the technical engineers, disappeared in the late 1960s when the studios took a less formal approach with its staff and how they appeared to clients. Today the department, now called Technical Services, works with technologies old and new. Abbey Road retains equipment spanning the duration of the Studio's existence as well as investing in the latest, cutting edge technology. Microphones from the 1930s and 1940s, compressor limiters and echo plates from the 1950s, four track analogue tape machines from the 1960s, mastering consoles from the 1970s, cutting lathes and analogue and digital tape machines from the 1980s, and early digital tape and workstation technology from the 1990s and 2000s are all still used on a regular basis today. These items, alongside all the contemporary equipment, are maintained by the Technical Services department.

On the audio engineering side there was a rigid hierarchy – at the top came the producer, who was responsible for managing a recording session. Next came the audio engineer with an assistant engineer charged with running the tape machine and sharing the workload. The common path was to start in the library, move onto disc cutting, followed by tape operation, and finally to work as an audio engineer. The broad structure of the engineering team survives today although producers and engineers no longer have to be members of EMI or Abbey Road staff. This condition outlasted the stipulation that only EMI artists record at Abbey Road, showing the significance of the engineers.

Opposite: *Engineers work in Studio 1 in the 1960s*
Right: *Technicians Keith Slaughter, Arthur Pook, and Bill Chow work in Control Room 1*

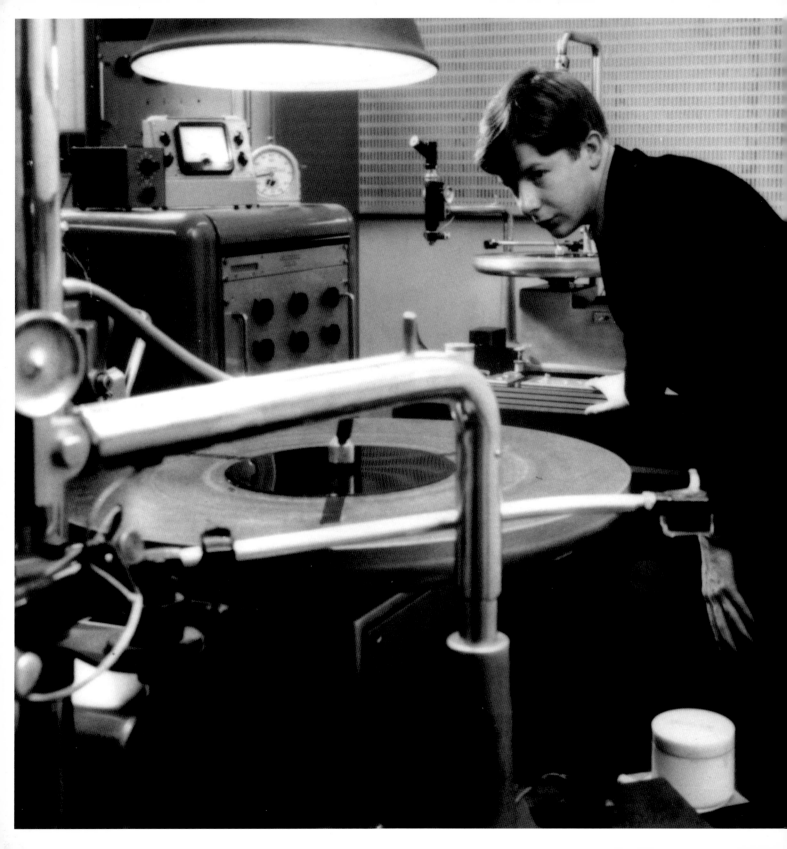

Ken Scott

Opposite: *A young Ken Scott in one of the Abbey Road cutting rooms, circa 1965*

Above: *Ken Scott, still a prominent music industry figure*

One of those who did manage the challenging rise from assistant engineer to producer at Abbey Road was Ken Scott. He joined the staff in 1963, aged 16, working in the tape library – a common job for new recruits. In the recording studios themselves, Scott's first assignment in 1964 was to assist on the early Beatles album *A Hard Day's Night*. He maintained his connection with the group as audio engineer on the albums *Beatles for Sale, Help!, Rubber Soul, Sgt. Pepper's Lonely Hearts Club Band, Magical Mystery Tour* and *'White Album'* – one of only five engineers to work with the band. Following the demise of The Beatles, and Scott's departure to Trident Studios (also in London), George Harrison requested his services as engineer on his debut solo album of 1970, *All Things Must Pass*. He also worked with John Lennon and Ringo Starr on various early solo projects.

Ken Scott's reputation as a platinum-selling producer was sealed over the coming decade with a number of high-profile rock albums produced at other studios, most famously several albums by iconic glam-rocker David Bowie, which included his mould-breaking concept LP *The Rise and Fall of Ziggy Stardust* of 1972. Scott has always acknowledged his debt to Abbey Road, where he learned his trade, reflecting the Studios' ability to provide great opportunities to talented young audio engineers. "At Abbey Road you followed your predecessors, who had determined the best place for everything," he told *Premier Guitar* magazine in 2010.

Every session was set up exactly the same way, at least to start with. On occasion we changed it slightly, but what they spent years finding out was normally the best.

Ken Scott, *Premier Guitar*, **2010**

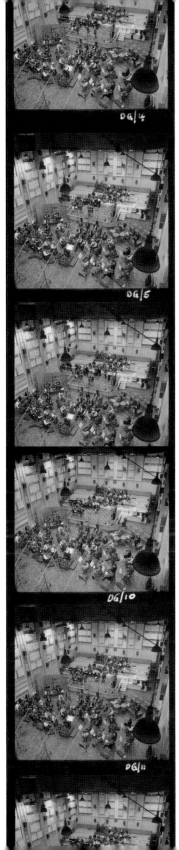

The classics
continue to thrive

Although it was put in the uncomfortable position of having to compete with pop, classical music continued to be recorded at Abbey Road during the 1960s, despite its public profile being diminished by the popularity of its younger, more lucrative rival.

One artist on EMI's Columbia roster who helped carry the flag for classical music was British pianist John Ogdon. In 1962 he consolidated his reputation as an international performer when he won first prize International Tchaikovsky Competition in Moscow. A series of recordings for HMV at Abbey Road followed, which included Mendelssohn and most famously Rachmaninov. Unfortunately Ogdon's career was blighted by mental health problems, but even with that hindrance to his productivity he wrote more than 200 of his own compositions for a number of instruments before his death in 1989. Today he is fondly remembered as a prodigious, proficient talent with a remarkable legacy.

Opposite: *John Ogdon, famed for being able to play most pieces at sight, plays piano in Studio 1*
Left: *Otto Klemperer conducts musicians from London's Philharmonia Orchestra in Studio 1*

Klemperer's comeback

Otto Klemperer had established himself as one of the world's leading classical conductors and composers as far back as the 1920s. A German-born Jew, he left his homeland with the rise of the Nazis, and held a number of high-profile positions in opera houses across Europe and the USA. After failing to settle in Hungary, and in ill health following the earlier removal of a brain tumour, Klemperer continued to relocate in search of a musical base. Finally settled in Switzerland, he sometimes worked at the Royal Opera House in London's Covent Garden, and signed to EMI in 1954. He made an immediate impact with a string of Beethoven symphonies recorded with London's Philharmonia Orchestra, founded by Walter Legge in 1945. In 1959, Klemperer was appointed the orchestra's first principal conductor and continued to record with them, and at Abbey Road. His career revived, Klemperer issued the best-selling records of his life with the Philharmonia for Columbia until his death in 1973.

Abbey Road royalty

The longest duration of a recording contract in the music industry is held between Yehudi Menuhin and EMI, whose relationship spanned almost 70 years until Menuhin's death at nearly 83 in 1999. First signed to HMV aged 13 in 1929, the childhood prodigy was already known on the classical circuit. Gifted a priceless 1773 Stradivarius violin for his 12th birthday from the banker and art collector Henry Goldman – co-founder of Goldman Sachs – he moved from New York to Europe with his family. Menuhin first played as a soloist at Abbey Road in the year of its creation, 1931, and the following year recorded an iconic version of Elgar's **Violin Concerto in B Minor** with Elgar himself conducting the London Symphony Orchestra.

Over Menuhin's lengthy career at Abbey Road, he experienced all the technological advances at first hand – in particular the move to magnetic tape recordings, which allowed for multiple takes and refinement. He clearly felt some nostalgia for early recordings, recalling a romantic quality he thought lost in the modern search for clarity and precision.

By the 1960s, public recognition of Menuhin's genius conferred upon him the title of honorary Knight Commander of the Order of the British Empire. His exclusive contract was renewed even when it became rare for EMI to maintain classical artists. This enduring relationship, and his commercial success, made him one of the company's most eminent and distinguished artists.

Above, left to right:
Menuhin records with acclaimed flautist Elaine Shaffer at Abbey Road; A Yehudi Menuhin promotional shot
Main: *Menuhin plays the violin in Studio 1*

Boult's encore and Schwarzkopf's final act

Two more classical artists whose careers benefited from time spent in the Studios during the 1960s were English conductor Sir Adrian Boult and German soprano Elisabeth Schwarzkopf. Boult served as director of music at the BBC for 20 years until 1950, when he reached retirement age and was forced to vacate his post. Age was no barrier to him recording, though, and he continued to work with several major orchestras in London. During the impressive later period of his career – known as his 'Indian summer' – Boult both revived the fortunes of the London Philharmonic Orchestra and resumed recording with EMI in 1964, after a six-year absence from the label.

Schwarzkopf extrapolated herself from the fallout of the Second World War – defending her membership of the Nazi party as a means of survival, it having been a condition of her contract at Berlin's Deutsches Opernhaus. In 1946 in Vienna she auditioned for EMI producer Walter Legge, was signed on an exclusive contract, and married Legge in 1953. An established star by the 60s, Schwarzkopf made several landmark recordings at Abbey Road before retiring in 1975. These included singing Donna Elvira in the famous recording of Mozart's **Don Giovanni** conducted by Giulini, and distinguished renditions of **Lieder** by Schubert, Brahms and especially Hugo Wolf.

Above: *Adrian Boult conducts a Vaughan Williams symphony in Studio 1*
Right: *Elisabeth Schwarzkopf is accompanied by Gerald Moore at Abbey Road*

> I love the physical thing of being on the earth that bore you. I have the same feeling when I walk in a very beautiful place that I have when I play and it goes right.

Jacqueline du Pré

Barenboim and du Pré: a classical couple

One of the most famous husband and wife teams in classical music history, Argentine conductor and pianist Daniel Barenboim and his wife, the prodigiously talented British cellist Jacqueline du Pré, recorded at Abbey Road during the 1960s. Both musicians started learning their craft at a young age. Barenboim began playing the piano at five, while du Pré was taught simple pieces on the cello by her mother, professional pianist and teacher Iris Greep du Pré, from the age of four. Barenboim recorded virtuoso performances of the complete Beethoven sonatas at the Studios, and also collaborated with du Pré, often in his guise as conductor. At just 20 years old, Du Pré's reputation as an international classical music star was enhanced by her keynote recording for EMI of Elgar's *Cello Concerto* under Sir John Barbirolli with the London Symphony Orchestra, which has remained in print ever since its release in 1965. Her other recordings in Studio 1 included compositions by Haydn, Richard Strauss, Beethoven, and Brahms. Greatly in demand, she toured the world performing with the leading conductors and orchestras of the day. Tragically, du Pré's tenure as a performer was cut short with the onset of multiple sclerosis in 1974. Barenboim made the transition to conducting operas in the 1970s and has become a highly regarded, award-winning music director.

Above: *(top) Barenboim records in Studio 1 with EMI producer Suvi Raj Grubb;*
(below and left) Barenboim works with viola player Cecil Aronowitz
Left: *Barenboim and du Pré share a moment of levity during an Abbey Road recording session*

Beyond the fringe

omedy recording continued to thrive at Abbey Road during the 1960s, championed and driven by George Martin, as it had been in the 1950s. Additions to the EMI roster of British talent included the cast of **Beyond the Fringe** – a popular satirical revue that ran in London and New York. Until 1968, all sketches from the show had to be vetted by the Lord Chamberlain before public performance. Written and performed by Oxbridge graduates Peter Cook, Dudley Moore, Alan Bennett, and Jonathan Miller, it was the original model for the genre that continues to poke fun at institutions such as parliament and the royal family. The young Ken Dodd – something of a throwback to the days of music hall comics – was also signed. He excelled at rapid-fire gags, sprinkled with songs in a light baritone. Dodd's **Tears** single from 1965 sold over a million copies.

In a completely different style, Peter Sellers was now in his prime. His 1965 album **Songs for Swingin' Sellers** featured a number of collaborations, including a duet with English comedy actress Irene Handl on the track **Shadows on the Grass**. Two other notable acts were slapstick artists Charlie Drake and Norman Wisdom, who separately made the transition to comedy records. Drake preceded his recordings with a successful TV career before developing the two in tandem, later moving into serious dramatic roles. Wisdom remained a light entertainer, having built up a fan base with a series of low-budget comedy films in the 50s.

Opposite, main:
Dudley Moore performs in Studio 2, watched by Peter Cook, Jonathan Miller, and others

Insets, left to right:
*The cast of **Beyond the Fringe**: Peter Cook, Alan Bennett, Dudley Moore, and Jonathan Miller; Ken Dodd; Irene Handl and Peter Sellers sing a duet; Charlie Drake; Norman Wisdom in Studio 1, 1964*

Top left: *David Frost in between takes while recording* **That Was The Week That Was**
Top right: **TW3** *performer Lance Percival*
Below: *George Martin talks to David Frost and Millicent Martin*
Opposite: *Leslie Phillips in Studio 2*

Satire and innuendo

Sometimes referred to as 'the satire boom', the 1960s provided fresh openings for a new breed of comedian, inspired by the success of **Beyond the Fringe**. A controversial hit on both sides of the Atlantic, **That Was The Week That Was** (known as **TW3**) was first aired on British television in late 1962. Written and directed by Ned Sherrin, it was presented by David Frost with input from Millicent Martin, Lance Percival, Roy Kinnear, Willie Rushton, and others. Some of those implicated went on to found satirical magazine **Private Eye**. The topical TV show was a revelation, lambasting taboo subjects such as religion, politics, and even the BBC. Unsure of how to deal with this potent material, the BBC cancelled the programme in 1964 deeming it unsuitable for broadcast during an election year. David Frost took the concept to America, where it won new acclaim with a fresh pool of local talent. It was no surprise that comedy fan George Martin signed the original **TW3** team.

Traditional British comedy survived at Abbey Road through entertainers such as Leslie Phillips. His career started on stage in the 1950s, and by the 60s he was an established film and TV actor, known for his upper-class persona, with roles in the first three **Carry On** films and two episodes of the BBC's **Comedy Playhouse**. Phillips' trademark public-school drawl was actually the result of elocution work on his original Cockney twang.

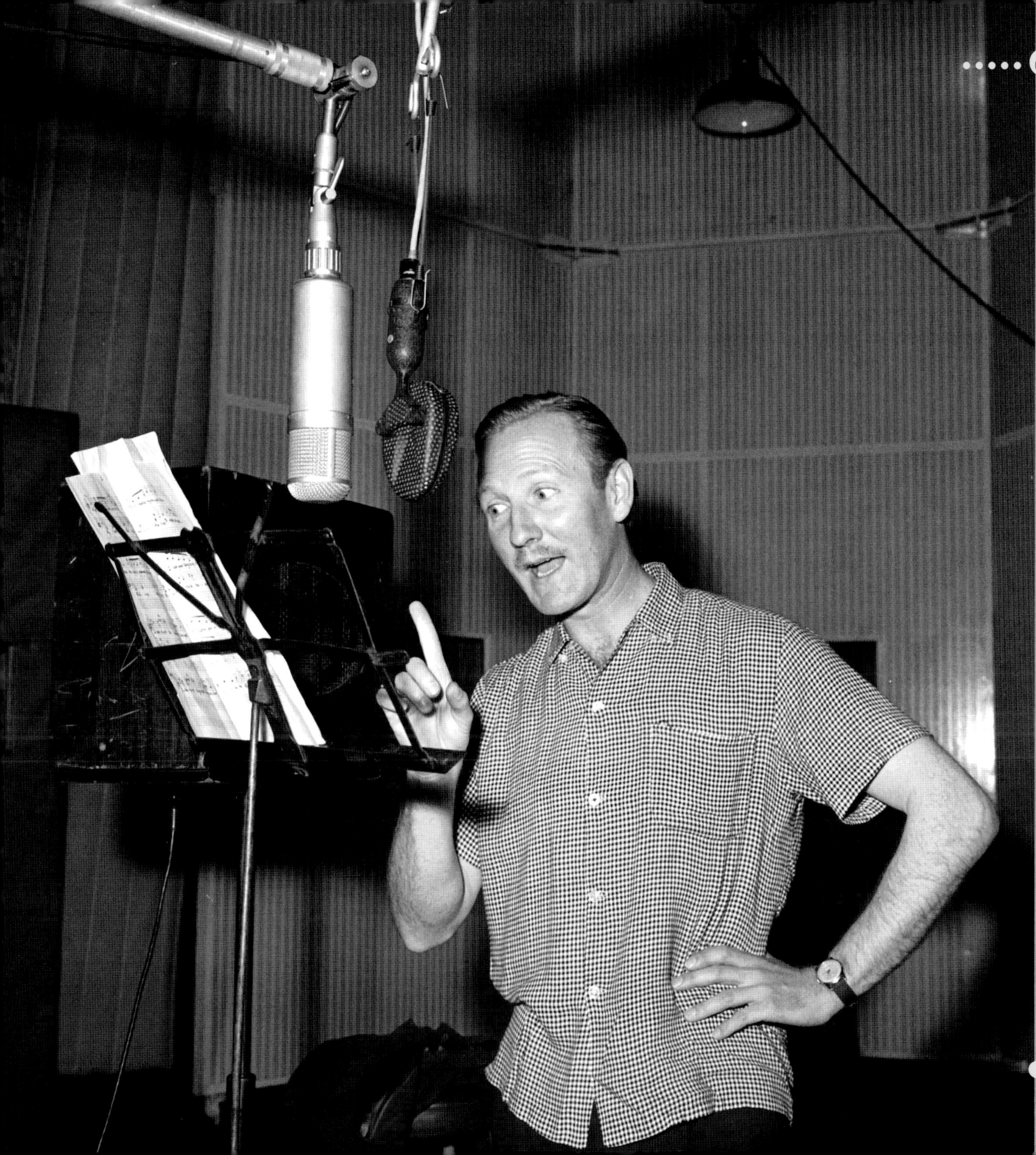

Eric, Ernie, and Abbey Road

Eric Morecambe and Ernie Wise were the undisputed kings of light entertainment in Britain during the 1960s. Established in 1961, the pair's prime-time television variety show moved to the BBC in 1968, where their popularity continued to rise. One Christmas special had a reported audience of 28 million viewers. Their routine consisted of sketches, physical comedy, their odd-couple act, musical numbers, and guest appearances.

The duo recorded their first comedy album, **Mr Morecambe Meets Mr Wise**, at the Studios in 1964 with producer Walter Ridley and an orchestra directed by Harry Robinson and Ken Thorne. It was released on the Music for Pleasure label – a joint venture between EMI and British publisher Hamlyn. **Mr Morecambe Meets Mr Wise** was a mix of sketches and songs, with a spurious credit on its front cover that 'Their Guest Star Erico Morecambeovicz even plays the **Greig Piano Concerto**'. This referred to a track with Morecambe playing an inept concert pianist. The sketch was later revised for one of their most famous TV sketches in which pianist, composer, and conductor André Previn – introduced in traditionally erroneous fashion as 'Andrew Preview' – conducted the bumbling Morecambe. The latter's unapologetic punchline "I'm playing all the right notes, but not necessarily in the right order" is one of his most well-known.

The Beatles provided another link to Abbey Road when they appeared on Morecambe and Wise's television show in December 1963. The hosts conducted a mock interview with the band before a performance of **Moonlight Bay**, which included John Lennon, Paul McCartney, and George Harrison quoting back many of Morecambe and Wise's catchphrases to them. All the time Ringo was stranded at the back of the stage behind his drum kit, addressed as 'Bongo' and 'Bonzo' by Morecambe throughout.

Right: *A series of shots showing Ernie Wise and Eric Morecambe recording in Studio 2*
Opposite: *Morecambe and Wise perform in the studio as Geoff Emerick watches from upstairs in the control room*

Bring me sunshine, in your smile. Bring me laughter, all the while. In this world where we live, there should be more happiness...

Bring Me Sunshine, **signature tune for** *The Morecambe and Wise Show* **from 1969**

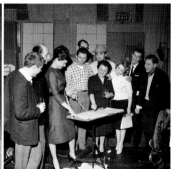

A dramatic twist

Two 'plays with music', as opposed to traditional musicals, were recorded at Abbey Road during the 1960s. In 1965, the Music for Pleasure label released an abridged version of Lewis Carroll's children's classic **Alice in Wonderland**. EMI man Norman Newell initially wrote the lyrics as a stage play, which then had the musical score supplied by film composer Philip Green. The all-star cast of British entertainers included Frankie Howerd and Tommy Cooper, who starred as the Mock Turtle and Mad Hatter, respectively, while Dirk Bogarde narrated.

A transfer from the stage to the recording studio, **Fings Ain't Wot They Used T'Be** enjoyed a successful run in London's West End when it opened in 1960. Pop and musical songwriter Lionel Bart scored Frank Norman's play about characters from London's underclass, replete with a dialogue and lyrics that made heavy use of cockney rhyming slang. A version of the title song was recorded for Parlophone as a novelty single by Lay-A-Bahts – a group invented for the purpose. Max Bygraves also had success with the track at Decca.

Maurice Chevalier
French charmer

A n EMI recording artist since the 1920s, Maurice Chevalier's career as an actor and singer spanned over five decades. He was one of a small élite to record at Abbey Road whose career had started before the Studios opened for business in 1931.

Chevalier sings for the screen

Born in 1888 in Paris, Chevalier and his older brother were circus acrobats before he landed his first singing job at age eleven. During the First World War, Chevalier was wounded and held as a prisoner of war in Germany for two years. In the Second World War, he agreed to perform to prisoners at the camp in which he had been interned, in exchange for the release of ten inmates. Between wars, meanwhile, Chevalier had become a huge international star. In fact, Chevalier was so famous that his passport featured in a running joke during the Marx Brothers, 1931 film **Monkey Business**.

Issued by HMV in 1929, his single **Louise**, backed with **On Top of the World**, was the first to complement a movie with songs and dialogue for the public to enjoy at home. This new strategy gave record companies the means to recoup revenue lost to the talkies.

Having survived a charge of collaboration with the Nazis in 1944, Chevalier was ironically refused entry to the United States in the McCarthy era because of his Communist sympathies. His career there was rekindled in 1954 with a US tour, then headlining in more Hollywood musicals – most famously 1958's **Gigi**. The album art for Pink Floyd's 1969 double album **Ummagumma** shows the soundtrack for **Gigi** leaning against the wall in some pressings. It was deleted on the US version due to copyright issues.

Right and opposite: *Maurice Chevalier records his song from* **Gigi** *in Studio 1, 1962*

Ella Fitzgerald loves The Beatles

Opposite and above:

'Queen of Jazz'
Ella Fitzgerald and
fellow musicians record
in Studio 2

Already an international star by the time she recorded at Abbey Road in the 1960s, legendary jazz vocalist Ella Fitzgerald's three-octave range marked her as a unique talent. Her series of **Songbook** albums recorded with Norman Granz's independent jazz label Verve between 1956 and 1964 featured covers of hits from outstanding American composers such as Cole Porter and Rodgers & Hart. Fitzgerald's 1957 collaboration with Duke Ellington won her the Grammy award for best jazz performance by a soloist, while her album of Irving Berlin songs in 1958 won the award for best female pop vocal performance – the first two of thirteen Grammies of her career.

In the 1960s Fitzgerald's dedication to covering new artists brought her to Abbey Road, which she insisted be the venue for her version of Lennon and McCartney's **Can't Buy Me Love** – so that it shared the birthplace of the original. Fitzgerald's rendition is remarkable as the first jazz version of the song, which has been covered nearly 40 times since its original release in 1964. Other interpretations were recorded by EMI alumni such as Peter Sellers, The King's Singers, and even George Martin – who released his **Off the Beatle Track** instrumental album with his orchestra, also in 1964.

Shirley Bassey's breakout

Shirley Bassey's strong, soulful voice established her as a star in the early 1950s and she had several chart hits with the Philips label, for whom she had been recording since 1956. Signed to EMI's Columbia label in 1959 at the age of 22, it was a coup for EMI to poach this major star and she became part of the EMI's stable of pop acts dominating the charts in the first half of the 1960s. Bassey scored hit upon hit – her deal with Columbia allowing her to record covers from musicals such as *Oliver!* as well as original material. Her career at Columbia was kick-started with her 1959 debut album *The Fabulous Shirley Bassey*, recorded with British easy-listening maestro Geoff Love and his Orchestra. Produced by George Martin and Norman Newell, the latter was also instrumental in recruiting American composer and bandleader Nelson Riddle, whom Bassey admired, for her well-received 1962 album *Let's Face the Music*.

One of the first black British singers to achieve national and international acclaim, Shirley Bassey enjoyed a string of early hits, including a thirty-week run in the singles charts with *As Long As He Needs Me* in 1960 – a song from the hit musical *Oliver!* Her cover of the popular French ballad *Et Maintenant* – retitled *What Now My Love?* – proved another triumph two years later.

Mainstream success in the United States, which had proved elusive, came with Bassey's powerful rendition of the title song for the 1964 James Bond movie *Goldfinger*, bringing her only *Billboard* hit – although she continued to sell out in concert. The single charted outside the Top 20 in the UK, but raised her profile another notch regardless.

Bassey left EMI as her chart success tailed off, and signed to the label United Artists. Her relationship with Abbey Road was not over, though. Her 1970 cover version of *Something* by The Beatles formed the title track of the first album of her renaissance, signalling her renewed presence in the UK charts. Many of Bassey's albums with United Artists were reissued by EMI after its acquisition of the label in 1979.

Right: *Shirley Bassey records at Abbey Road with producer George Martin*
Opposite: *A promotional shot from the 1960s*

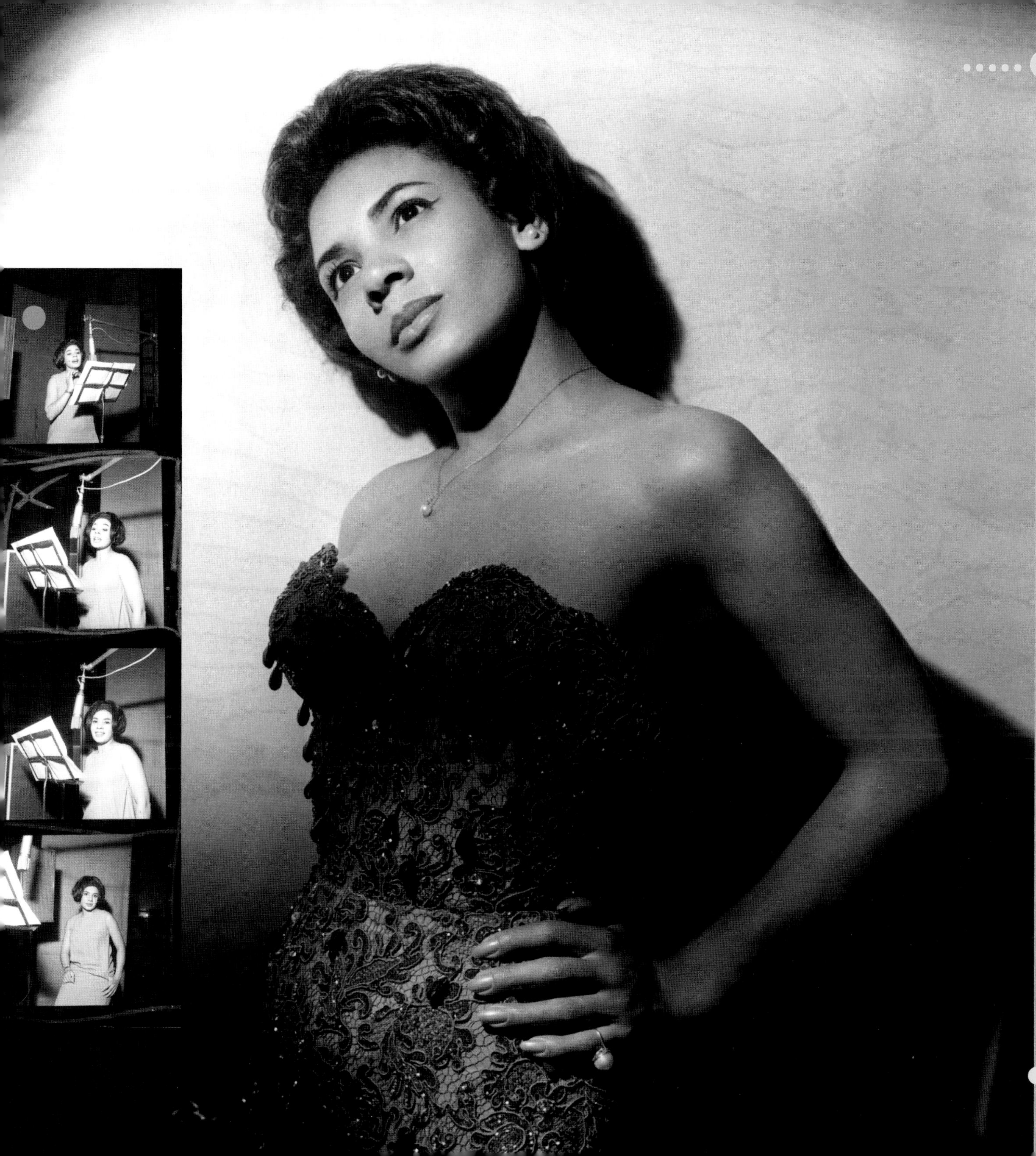

Below and opposite:

Relaxed recording sessions with Matt Monro, George Martin, and musical director Johnnie Spence

Output from Abbey Road in the 1960s did not just break new artists – it also brought one back from obscurity. Singer Matt Monro had been given exposure in the 1950s during the boom period for young male vocalists who sang the standards, but by the following decade his star had waned.

George Martin revived Monro's career when he recruited him to help Peter Sellers imitate Frank Sinatra's easy-listening croon on the comedian's ***Songs For Swinging Sellers*** album in 1960. Sellers was so impressed with Monro's vocals on the satirical number ***You Keep Me Swingin'*** that he chose his version to open the album. Although billed under the pseudonym Fred Flange, Monro's true identity came out and it was enough to reignite his prospects. Martin signed him to Parlophone and a number of hits in Britain and the United States followed. Among them was a commission to sing a theme song for the new film franchise James Bond – 1963's ***From Russia with Love***.

"His pitch was right on the nose, his word enunciations letter perfect, his understanding of a song thorough."

Frank Sinatra pays tribute to Matt Monro

Pop comes of age

erhaps the most successful solo performer to emerge from Abbey Road, Cliff Richard signed with EMI in the late 50s alongside his backing band The Drifters, who later changed their name to The Shadows. Signed by Norrie Paramor to the Columbia label, the teenage Cliff Richard and The Shadows recorded their early releases in Studio 2 under the producer's guidance. "The strange thing was I couldn't sing without the guitar, even though I never played it very well," Richard told the authors of the 2002 book **Abbey Road**, when asked about his first session. "It wasn't working out too well and Norrie suggested I put the guitar on and it all just happened." "Hearing our guitars and voices after those first sessions, we were totally overawed," recalled his band mate Bruce Welch. "We could hardly play and everything was so simple and then when we heard it back there seemed to be so much going on."

Part of the UK's embrace of rock and roll, Richard's appeal was tested by the arrival of the Merseybeat bands. His popularity served him well, though, and he was able to survive despite being viewed by some as out of fashion, or 'square'. He recorded seven No. 1 singles in the 1960s, and songs such as 1962's **The Young Ones** and 1963's **Summer Holiday** reached classic status.

Opposite, from left: *Bruce Welch, Brian Bennett, Hank Marvin, Brian 'Licorice' Locking, and Cliff Richard lark about behind despairing engineer Malcolm Addey*
Below: *Cliff and The Shadows during recording sessions with Malcolm Addey*
Right: *Cliff and The Shadows in portrait*

Above and opposite:

*Adam Faith records a live show for the BBC programme **Drumbeat** in Studio 2*

An all-rounder whose career took flight in 1959 with his first No. 1, **What Do You Want**, Adam Faith was a true anomaly. Following brief signings to HMV and Top Rank, he was one of the first pop acts signed to Parlophone, and the first pop musician to appear on one of the early episodes of long-running BBC current affairs programme **Face to Face**, where the then 20-year-old held his own against the Archbishop of York. Faith showed himself as a very different type of pop star.

Parlophone had taken a punt and signed Faith, having spotted his regular appearances in 1959 on the short-lived BBC music series **Drumbeat**, alongside The John Barry Seven. A high-profile film role followed with **Beat Girl** in 1960 – Faith both starred and featured on the soundtrack. Composed by John Barry, this was the first British film soundtrack to be issued on LP (on the Columbia label). The movie's themes of youth rebellion contrast with the more anodyne teen pop that typified Faith's later recorded output over the 1960s. Adam Faith went on to release six albums for Parlophone in five years, and was the first pop artist to reach the Top Five with all of his first seven hits. He collaborated frequently with Barry, whose inventive arrangements of standards and modern songs marked out Faith's debut album, **Adam**, for wide acclaim.

Originally billed as a rival to Cliff Richard, Faith could not sustain his popularity in the face of The Beatles' success. He recorded only two albums between 1974 and 1993, making the transition into music management during the 1970s as mentor to Leo Sayer. Unexpectedly, Faith turned in the 1980s to somewhat unsuccessful financial investment advice and financial journalism. He then revived his acting career, starring in a string of TV drama series in Britain until the early 2000s.

John Barry flourishes

Originally a 1950s rock and roll musician, John Barry disbanded his group – The John Barry Seven – in favour of becoming a music arranger for EMI. It was a transition that paid off handsomely, as his work at Abbey Road helped establish Barry as one of the most acclaimed composers of the 20th century.

Barry's first foray into film music was with *Beat Girl* in 1960, composing, arranging, and conducting the score. The film was a vehicle for EMI artist Adam Faith, with whom Barry had previously worked on some of his pop recordings. The pair also shared an A&R manager in Norman Newell.

Two years later, Barry received his big break when asked to re-arrange the theme for the first film in the James Bond franchise: *Dr. No*. The result was one of the most iconic theme tunes in film history, and Barry went on to compose 11 further Bond themes. He was also an innovator, being one of the first to employ synthesizers in a film score – *On Her Majesty's Secret Service* – and to make wide use of pop artists and songs, as he did in *Midnight Cowboy.* He did not, however, abandon the archetypal film score of classical musicians working within a traditional orchestral arrangement.

" Golden words he will pour in your ear, but his lies can't disguise what you fear

For a golden girl knows when he's kissed her, it's the kiss of death from Mister Goldfinger. "

Goldfinger, **1964, score by John Barry, lyrics by Leslie Bricusse and Anthony Newley**

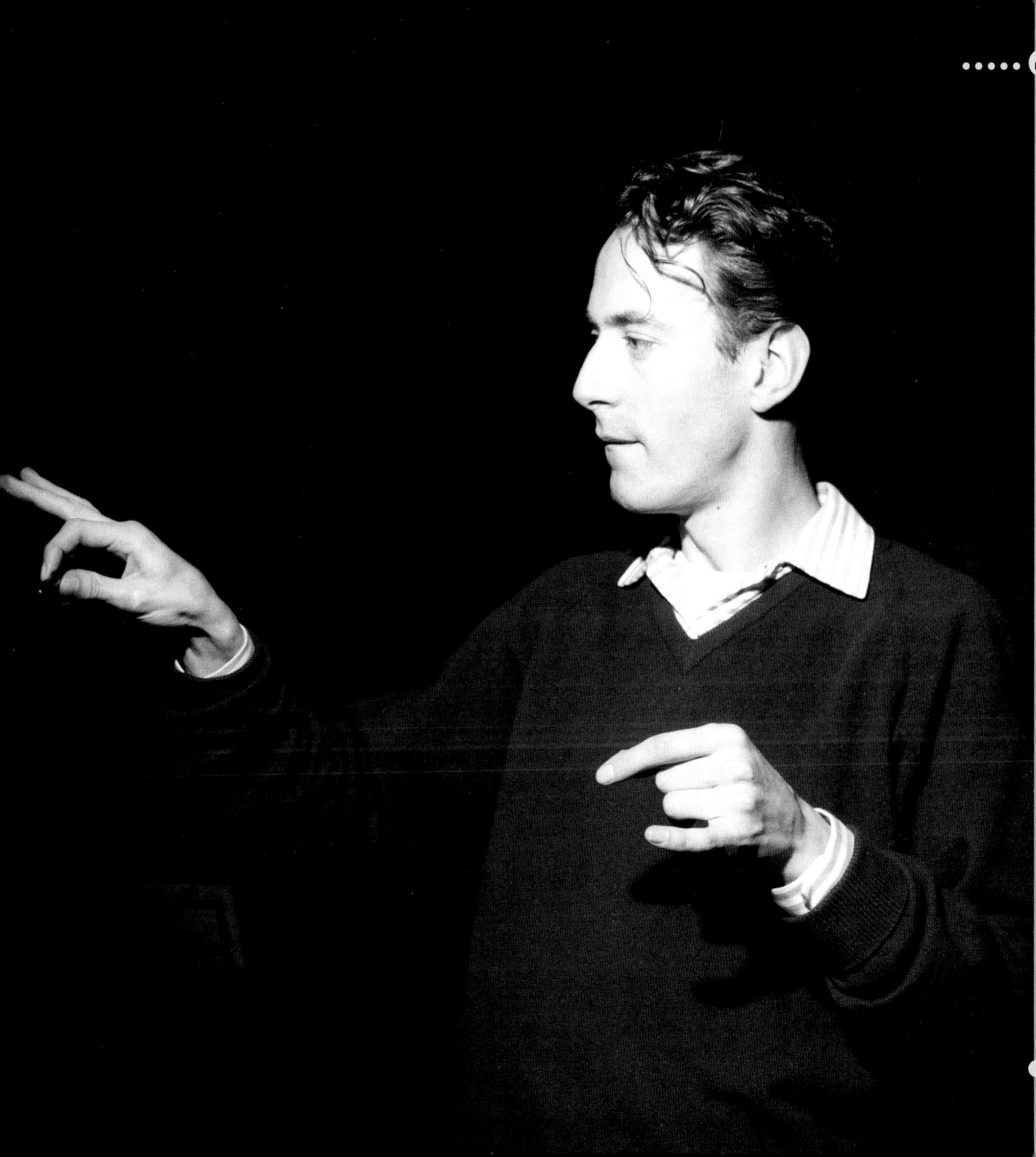

London-born singer Helen Shapiro was another female solo talent to emerge from Abbey Road. Signed to Columbia at just 14 because of her mature, throaty vocals, she became a teenage star when she released her first single, **Don't Treat Me like a Child**, in 1961. Working with producer Norrie Paramor, Shapiro enjoyed several years of prosperity before her popularity declined. Ironically her beehive hairdo and singing style were seen as outmoded, despite the fact she was still younger than many of her peers. The Beatles wrote **Misery** for her, but it was declined on her behalf – something she later cited as a missed opportunity.

One group whose career took an unorthodox trajectory were British R&B singer Cliff Bennett and his band The Rebel Rousers. Under producer Joe Meek, their early recordings were leased to Parlophone but failed to make an impact. The group spent several years mainly touring Germany, where they met The Beatles in Hamburg. The latter recommended them to their manager Brian Epstein, who signed them in the mid-60s. In 1966, Cliff Bennett and The Rebel Rousers finally charted with a cover of the Beatles' **Got to Get You into My Life**, produced by Paul McCartney. Their star had waned by the early 70s, and Bennett gradually retired from the music industry. He became an unlikely shipping magnate, though later returned to touring with various line-ups.

> The best years of my life I know are those when I am young
>
> And since I'm sure that this is so, gonna have my fun.

Helen Shapiro, *Don't Treat Me Like a Child***, 1961**

Right: *Stills from the cover shoots for Helen Shapiro's* **Helen Hits Out!** *and* **Got to Get You into Our Life** *by Cliff Bennett and the Rebel Rousers*
Opposite: *A publicity shot of the teenage Helen Shapiro from the early 60s*

n the BEATLE'S track

RECORD MAIL'S Photo-Feature this month goes out and about with The Beatles and it will not take Liverpool fans long to recognise familiar Cavern Club surrounds (above) which saw much of their early success. The remaining pictures (all taken by Mail staff photographer JOHN DOVE), show the boys further south—in London for a recording session at E.M.I.'s St. John's Wood studios, and to have their photographs taken for an LP sleeve (extreme right). The bemused 'bobby' obviously wondered what it was all about! Drummer Ringo Starr (left) feels on top of the world—whether he likes it or not and (right) you might think that Paul McCartney, George Harrison and John Lennon are having a joke at Ringo's expense. Actually they're changing for photographs. There's Parlophone recording manager George Martin (far right) looking on as George Harrison tries out some chords and buttons right; he joins the boys for a cuppa after some hard work in the studios, a successful session completed. The Beatles are pictured (centre) leaving the studios—off, no doubt, to conquer fresh fields. And, talking of conquering, they're doing just that with their latest 'single' (you can't keep it quiet!). The Beatles, too—"From me to you" is to be released shortly on Parlophone R5015.

NO need to tell you who these are! The chart-topping Beatles pictured here with Parlophone recording manager George

---

The latest 'Pop' EPs in Mono and Stereo

EXTENDED PLAY PRICE LIST

THE BEATLES
Please Please Me/Ask Me Why
PARLOPHONE 45-R4983

THE BEATLES crashed into the charts with their first release and to my mind this is a much better side . . . so it will be an even bigger hit. Playing and singing, they rock through the optimistic item on the top side. The unique sound made by the group, coupled with the lyric and memorable melody make

---

EATLES IN FOCUS

A TWO-PAGE Christmas present for Beatles' fans everywhere—four recent recording studio shots of John, George, Paul and Ringo, plus a great new group picture of them. There'll be a Happy Christmas, too, with the Beatles' new single, "I feel fine" (Parlophone R5200), and their LP "Beatles for sale," which is released this month on Parlophone PMC1240 (stereo, PCS3062).

RECORD MAIL

A MONTHLY REVIEW AND DETAILS OF THE LATEST 'POPULAR' RECORDS ISSUED BY E.M.I RECORDS
H.M.V, Capitol, Columbia, Parlophone, Encore, Stateside, M-G-M, Liberty, United Artists, Verve, Tamla Motown

Vol. 8 No. 8 (Published the first Friday of each month) August, 1965

HELP!

"**H**ELP!" cry the Beatles in their new film, recently premiered in London's West End. "Help!"—title song of the film—is on record, too (Parlophone R5305). And there's an LP containing more music from the film—on Parlophone PMC1255 (stereo PCS3071). (John Castle p.3)

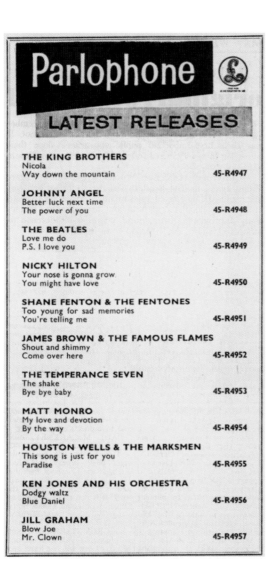

Almost abandoned

By the time The Beatles came to Abbey Road to record their first demo with George Martin on the evening of Wednesday 6 June 1962, they had already played more than 900 concerts in the UK and Germany. They had also been passed over by almost every record label in Britain.

  "They looked like four very likeable, long-haired lads from Liverpool, with great senses of humour." remembers Ken Townsend. "The session started and George [Martin] was considering abandoning it because there was a lot of distortion from the bass guitar," he continues. "He asked me if there was anything we could do, and I said the only speaker we had that was suitable was in one of the echo chambers – so Norman Smith and I brought it over. I wired a jack plug to an amplifier input and plugged it in, and it worked. I don't know why I just happened to have that amplifier on my desk, but I often look back now and wonder, if that hadn't happened – would The Beatles ever have been The Beatles?" he laughs.

  The band's own equipment was suitable for playing on stage but not in a studio. Martin and the engineers explained the problem to the band after the session – during which they recorded *Bésame Mucho*, *Ask Me Why*, *Love Me Do*, and *How Do You Do It?* It was the first of many consultations between the artists and their production team.

Opposite: *Cuttings featuring The Beatles from EMI's in-house magazine* **Record Mail** *dating from 1962 to 1965.* **Help!** *was the second Beatles movie – it was a comedy adventure, spoofing the Bond series and packed with surreal Goon Show-style humour.*
Left: *A cutting advertising The Beatles' first single, 1962's* **Love Me Do**, *with* **P.S. I Love You** *on the flip side*

The Beatles' demo session was the first and last appearance at Abbey Road of Pete Best. The band re-recorded **Love Me Do** on 4th September with Ringo drumming and again on 11 September with session drummer Andy White and Ringo playing tambourine. The original single was released with Ringo drumming while the album has the Andy White version, as do later pressings of the single.

Hitting the No. 1 spot

It took until the following year for No. 1 singles to arrive for The Beatles, when they managed three in quick succession – **From Me to You**, **She Loves You**, and **I Want to Hold Your Hand**. The Beatles were immediately set apart from their peers with by preference for recording their own compositions. The songwriting team of Lennon and McCartney would dominate the band's writing credits, and the pair became almost omnipresent in the Studios during the 60s. A host of other artists also covered Beatles songs or made commercial recordings of tracks discarded from the Fab Four's own recording sessions. In some cases, the pair wrote specifically for other artists, including The Rolling Stones.

The Beatles experiment

With their rise to superstardom, The Beatles made the most of their time in Abbey Road. As crowds of fans regularly gathered at the gates in an attempt to catch a glimpse of the quartet, the group worked long hours undisturbed within its walls. This divide was never watertight, though, as producer Norman Smith found on one occasion when he discovered two girls hiding in a cupboard – who then made a dash for a nearby Paul McCartney. Smith's professional remit was expanded to security as he was forced to eject the girls from the building.

The Beatles were not the first artists to work late into the night at Abbey Road, but they were the first to experiment extensively with its space. They recorded in cupboards, alcoves, and other unorthodox corners – purely to see what effects these would offer. This creativity and lateral thinking ran in parallel to the different musical styles they embraced. Many of these experiments occurred not just under the watchful eye, but also with the encouragement, of George Martin. He demonstrated his own talents through altering the tempo of the song **Please Please Me** from that of a ballad to a pop hit, and later lobbied to incorporate a string quartet on **Yesterday**.

The labyrinthine nature of the Studios building also allowed for some moments of escape – John Lennon in particular enjoyed trips to the roof to 'meditate', despite Martin's strong disapproval. One story of Lennon disappearing for more than an hour, and his bandmates retrieving him hurriedly and in a slight panic, has since passed into Abbey Road's folklore.

In stark contrast to their later, lengthier sessions at Abbey Road, The Beatles' first album, 1963's **Please Please Me**, was recorded in a mere 13 hours. This reflected their as yet undeveloped experience as recording artists – they had not begun to tinker with the nuances and inflections of each song. The group's success upgraded the status of Parlophone within EMI; it was the smallest and least prestigious of its three main labels until The Beatles' revolution elevated George Martin's work to hitherto unheard-of levels of commercial success.

HYPERSENSITIVE PANCHROMATIC

Opposite and above:
The Beatles photographed in Manchester Square, home of EMI headquarters at the time, and outside Abbey Road in March 1963 with George Martin and Brian Epstein
Right: *John, Paul, George, and Ringo in a recording session in Studio 2, 1964*

123

> "ADT came out of a genuine need. We had got so fed up with spending so much time adding voice after voice that Ken and I used to talk about it continually until one day he went off and invented it."

George Martin, *Abbey Road*, 2002

Just as The Beatles overturned traditional ways of working at Abbey Road, so too they urged its engineers to push the boundaries of the technology available. Audio engineer Ken Townsend came up with a bespoke technique to furnish the group with a richer sound. His Artificial Double Tracking (ADT) now made it possible to simulate two sets of vocals or instrumentals on a recording. Townsend worked at the Studios throughout his 42-year career, finally retiring as President.

The invention of ADT

Abbey Road introduced the first four-track machine in 1959, allowing elements of recordings to be split into separate tracks. It suited pop recordings, which generally had fewer instruments than classical recordings, so were easier to balance across four audio tracks. Musicians such as The Beatles revelled in its possibilities for experimentation. Early or 'manual' double tracking, however, required artists to sing or play along with their own pre-recorded performance to create a stronger sound than that of a single voice or instrument. Having spent long hours recording in the Studios, Lennon and his group now insisted on something new.

Townsend hit upon the idea of playing back two identical performances, with one slightly out of synch. He added a second tape recorder to the setup and routed the vocal track back with the speed and delay created and managed by an oscillator, varying the speed of the second tape. The two vocal tracks were then combined to create the double-tracked effect. The Beatles adopted ADT with relief and used it throughout their 1966 album *Revolver*.

Although a watershed moment in sound engineering, ADT did not replace manual double tracking entirely. Because ADT uses two identical tracks, some artists – The Beatles included – still preferred the manual method at times, depending on what textures they wanted for their recording. Nonetheless, it remains an undisputed masterstroke that changed the way in which studio sessions would be recorded forever. Multi-track recording still underpins modern recording, mastering, remastering, and remixing as it allows endless variation for sound to be modified in post-production.

Opposite: *Workers at EMI's factory in Hayes, Middlesex, pack copies of The Beatles'* **Hard Day's Night** *album – recorded using four-track technology*
Below: *The REDD mixing desk was used at Abbey Road during the period when Artificial Double Tracking was invented*

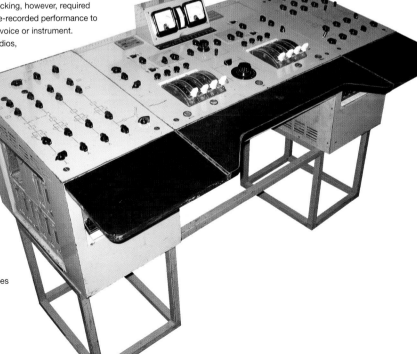

Opposite: *Billy J. Kramer (right) at the control desk with producer Norman Smith, who later went on to record his own hits under the pseudonym of Hurricane Smith*
Left: *Freddie and the Dreamers record in Studio 2; Frank Ifield poses for a publicity shot*

Chart toppers and the Merseybeat

1963 saw an unprecedented triumph for EMI and the Studios as their artists occupied the No. 1 spot in the UK singles chart for 23 consecutive weeks. Many of these artists were part of the 'Merseybeat' phenomenon – the name given to the tide of young acts from the north of the country – mainly Liverpool, on the River Mersey. The title may derive from the **Mersey Beat** magazine created by former art-school classmate of John Lennon, Bill Harry.

The Merseybeat sound ushered in a new era of pop and rock music. Influenced by 50s rock and roll from the United States, it also took elements from other North American genres such as skiffle, R&B, doo-wop, and soul. The new category could accommodate guitar bands as easily as singers of ballads, with The Beatles as undisputed royalty.

Epstein's influence

A key figure in the 1960s rebirth of British pop music was Beatles manager Brian Epstein. He managed a number of artists whose music eventually defined the period, such as fellow Liverpudlian singer Billy J. Kramer – a friend of John Lennon. Epstein shrewdly put Kramer together with a new backing band – The Dakotas, from Manchester. Keen to keep their own identity, the band signed separately to Parlophone under George Martin, as Billy J. Kramer with The Dakotas.

In 1963, Kramer covered **Do You Want to Know a Secret?** – a track from The Beatles' first album **Please Please Me**, released the same year. The track charted at No. 2, and John Lennon then wrote for Kramer his biggest hit **Bad to Me**, which led to his first No.1 in the UK and a Top Ten hit in the United States. Demos exist of Lennon playing the song in 1963, but it was never recorded by The Beatles. Kramer stepped out of The Beatles' shadow with his second No. 1 when he recorded **Little Children** rather than another Lennon–McCartney composition. During this period, George Martin also produced instrumental pieces by The Dakotas, including his own composition **Magic Carpet**.

Freddie and the Dreamers – another band consisting of a front man with a backing band – were also seen as part of the Merseybeat genre, though the group hailed from Manchester. They first tasted chart success with a cover version of American R&B singer James Ray's **If You Gotta Make a Fool of Somebody**, which debuted at No. 3 in 1963. This release is said to have led to some acrimony between them and The Beatles, as Paul McCartney alleged that the Dreamers' version was based on an arrangement The Beatles had played in a live performance at the Cavern Club in Liverpool. The rift was forgotten with the continued success of both artists, and Freddie and the Dreamers appeared as guests in The Beatles' 1964 Christmas Special at the Hammersmith Odeon.

Country and Western star

Separate from the Merseybeat group was Frank Ifield. A Country and Western vocalist, he was British-born but had emigrated to Australia with his family as a child and had fallen in love with 'hillbilly' music during his rural upbringing there. Established as a star in Australia and New Zealand by the mid-1950s, Ifield's path led him back to the UK and Abbey Road. Under producer Norrie Paramor from 1960, he made it into the UK charts with the single **Lucky Devil**, and his first No. 1 followed two years later with a Country version of the 1940s standard **I Remember You**, which sold more than a million copies and topped the charts for seven weeks.

Ifield's success continued through the 1960s. Surprisingly, he even shared an album release with the vastly different Beatles. The Liverpool quartet's lack of control over their original licensing deal in the United States led to the unlikely issue of **Jolly What! England's Greatest Recording Stars: The Beatles and Frank Ifield on Stage**. This compilation, issued exclusively in the US, parcelled together four previously released Beatles tracks with eight Ifield numbers. Less surprisingly, it was one of many Beatles compilations that were deleted when the group took control of their back catalogue.

Clockwise, from above: *Cover art for various albums and singles released by Abbey Road recording artists during the 1960s –* **Meet The Dakotas** *EP of 1963; the self-titled debut by Cliff Bennett and the Rebel Rousers, 1965; Billy J. Kramer's* **Little Children**, *1963;* **Close To You**, *1966, by Frank Ifield;* **Cinderella** *by Cliff Richard and The Shadows, 1967;* **Bridge on the River Wye**, *by Spike Milligan and Peter Sellers, with Peter Cook and Jonathan Miller, 1962;* **The Romantic Eartha** *by Eartha Kitt, 1962;* **Freddie and the Dreamers in Disneyland** *by Freddie and the Dreamers, 1966*

Opposite: *The cover for the soundtrack to* **Beat Girl**, *of 1961, starring pop idol Adam Faith and composed by John Barry*

Music from the film

'BEAT GIRL'

JOHN BARRY

ADAM FAITH

SHIRLEY ANNE FIELD

COLUMBIA
LONG PLAYING 33⅓ R.P.M. RECORD

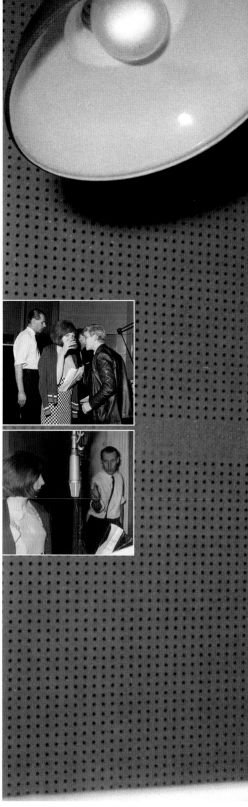

> "How do you do what you do to me, I wish I knew. If I knew how you do it to me, I'd do it to you.
>
> How do you do what you do to me, I'm feelin' blue. Wish I knew how you do it to me, but I haven't a clue."

How Do You Do It?, **Gerry and the Pacemakers, 1963**

George Martin picks more winners

In addition to producing his stable of top artists, George Martin continued to seek out fresh acts. Among these were young vocalists Cilla Black and Gerry Marsden – more icons of the Merseybeat revolution. Gerry and the Pacemakers, fronted by Marsden, was the second band to be signed by manager Brian Epstein after The Beatles; he also managed Black's career. Assigned to Columbia, the Pacemakers were launched with the song **How Do You Do It?** Previously turned down but eventually recorded by The Beatles, this was the first of a trio of No. 1 hits for the group – completed by **I Like It** and **You'll Never Walk Alone** – all issued in 1963. The latter, from the 1945 Rodgers and Hammerstein musical **Carousel**, became an anthem for Liverpool itself and sold over 750,000 copies. Adopted by fans of Liverpool FC, it is now sung across the world at association football fixtures. Marsden then wrote **Ferry Cross the Mersey** – the title track for their second album, and an explicit link to their heritage.

Another great George Martin discovery was British composer and conductor Ron Goodwin, who joined Parlophone in the 50s as a ghostwriter and accompanist. In 1960, Goodwin featured on Peter Sellers' **Goodness Gracious Me** album, establishing himself a year later with scores for four films in the Miss Marple franchise. In total, he scored more than 60 well-known movies, including **Where Eagles Dare** and **Battle of Britain**.

Above, from left: *George Martin with Gerry and the Pacemakers at Marsden's 21st birthday party;*
Gerry and the Pacemakers at Abbey Road; Three shots of Cilla Black in session with George Martin and colleagues
Opposite: *Cilla Black and George Martin set up for a recording at the Studios*

> " The road is long, with many a winding turn,
>
> That leads us to who knows where, Who knows where? "

The Hollies, *He Ain't Heavy, He's My Brother*

The Hollies – one of British rock music's longest-serving acts – also cut their teeth at Abbey Road during the 1960s. They signed to Parlophone in 1963 under the tutelage of Ron Richards, who at the time was George Martin's assistant engineer but also produced tracks by The Beatles and Gerry and The Pacemakers. Richards produced The Hollies during the 60s and 70s, during which time they recorded numerous hit singles in the UK, securing their first No. 1 spot with *I'm Alive* in 1965.

The more things change...

Unlike The Beatles, The Hollies preferred cover versions of American songs to writing their own material. *Searchin'*, *Stay*, and *Just One Look* – released as singles in 1963 and 1964 – were transplants of doo-wop and R&B numbers from the United States. This suited The Hollies' preference for close harmonies and a simplistic pop sensibility, the latter being something they only adopted once beginning to record at Abbey Road.

"Ron Richards never tried to change our style because we had a pretty distinctive sound, but he did help me to play simpler," Tony Hicks told the authors of *Abbey Road* in 1982. "I was putting too many notes in, which is something a lot of people do before they have actually recorded in a studio... When you hear it played back on tape, it sounds an absolute jumble."

The group's dedication to a straightforward approach meant that while others experimented with new technologies and techniques, The Hollies preferred to utilize few overdubs. However, they were not above experimenting with what sounds they could capture on tape in the Studios during their early days recording there.

"One day [vocalist] Allan Clarke sang in Studio 2 with a bass drum over his head to create some particular sound we wanted," remembered Hicks. "Once, we had everybody banging bottles together, kicking doors, and scratching walls to make a sort of manic sound." Five decades later, The Hollies are still recording and touring.

Right, top to bottom: *The Hollies record at Abbey Road in 1965*
Opposite: *The front cover of The Hollies' self-titled album, released in 1965*

HOLLIES

A very British invasion

The so-called 'British Invasion' of the 1960s saw UK acts invade the United States Billboard charts, in contrast to the usual state of play where the British hit parade was dominated by US hits. Barriers in pop music were dismantled forever, and Abbey Road – the factory that created many of these hits – was put squarely on the map.

The Studios became a recording venue for increasing numbers of international stars, such as songwriter and performer Burt Bacharach and one of the twentieth century's biggest stars – actress and singer Judy Garland.

Alongside such arrivals, the original mélange of domestic pop and genre musicians continued to thrive within the Studios' walls. British jazz band The Temperance Seven recorded George Martin's first No. 1 hit with 1961's ***You're Driving Me Crazy***, while London-based R&B group Manfred Mann and pop duo Peter and Gordon added to the British Invasion's ranks. Vocalist Shane Fenton set out on his career – not yet transmogrified into his glam-rock persona as Alvin Stardust – and bluesy British rockers The Pretty Things hinted at what was to come.

Clockwise from left: *Manfred Mann with Burt Bacharach at the piano; Billy J. Kramer in the Abbey Road canteen; The Swinging Blue Jeans, who charted in the UK and the US in the mid-60s; The Pretty Things; The Temperance Seven; Eartha Kitt; Bruce Johnson; Aussie import Rolf Harris; Shane Fenton (right) with Eden Kane; Peter and Gordon*

The Beatles live from Abbey Road

The Studios helped achieve another first when, in 1967, The Beatles contributed to the first international satellite television production, live from Studio 1 as part of the programme *Our World*. This ambitious project showcased creative artists from 19 countries, and was viewed by close to 400 million people around the globe – the largest-ever TV audience at the time. The Beatles closed proceedings with a performance of *All You Need Is Love*, written by John Lennon for the occasion.

The Beatles' segment was intended to show the band at work on the song, but this was judged impractical. The tune was instead presented as finished, but was in fact a work in progress. Overdubs were used for part of the backing track, as the group sang live alongside a small orchestra. Some of the band's musician friends – including The Rolling Stones, Marianne Faithfull, and Eric Clapton – provided backing vocals for the chorus, but its call and response refrain was apparently improvised. Prior to recording there was only one rehearsal.

Another nod to the future was the colour photographs taken to document the event, which allowed the original black-and-white broadcast to be accurately 'colourized' in 1995, when it was used in the TV special *The Beatles Anthology*.

Opposite: *The Beatles rehearse in Studio 1 ahead of the* **Our World** *broadcast*
Left: *The Beatles prepare to perform live to a TV audience of some 400 million*

There's nothing you can do that can't be done, nothing you can sing that can't be sung... It's easy

All You Need Is Love, **The Beatles, 1967**

The fluid nature of collaborations at Abbey Road during the 1960s allowed several stars to establish themselves and flourish. In 1966, guitarist Jeff Beck left The Yardbirds – signed to EMI on the Columbia label – to pursue a solo career. In 1968 he and his own band, The Jeff Beck Group, released their seminal album **Truth** – also via Columbia.

Mickie Most was the producer on **Truth**, but delegated some of his role to sound engineer Ken Scott of Abbey Road, contributing mainly in the post-recording mixes. Most had worked with Beck in the past, and was a pop entrepreneur of some repute, having produced a string of hits in the 60s on both sides of the Atlantic. He was not an Abbey Road employee, but often booked recording space and cutting facilities there. He formed his own label, RAK, in 1968 and later established himself as a TV personality on the UK talent show **New Faces**.

Jeff Beck finds his metal

Unlike his previous work with Mickie Most, **Truth** indulged Beck's passion for hard rock and blues. Recorded in just four days at Abbey Road, it helped pave the way for the birth of heavy metal in the 70s. Many of its ten tracks were covers, but some were credited to Jeffrey Rod – a pseudonym for the songwriting team of Beck and the young Rod Stewart, who performed lead vocals. Completing the band's line-up were drummer Micky Walker and future Rolling Stones guitarist Ronnie Wood. Among the session musicians who contributed to the album was American soul singer Madeline Bell. Bell found fame in the UK in the 1960s, initially as a member of the pop group Blue Mink.

Above, left to right: *Jeff Beck; collaborators (from left) Rod Stewart, Jeff Beck, Ronnie Wood, and Aynsley Dunbar; producer Mickie Most*
Opposite: *Madeline Bell waits in one of Abbey Road's control rooms*

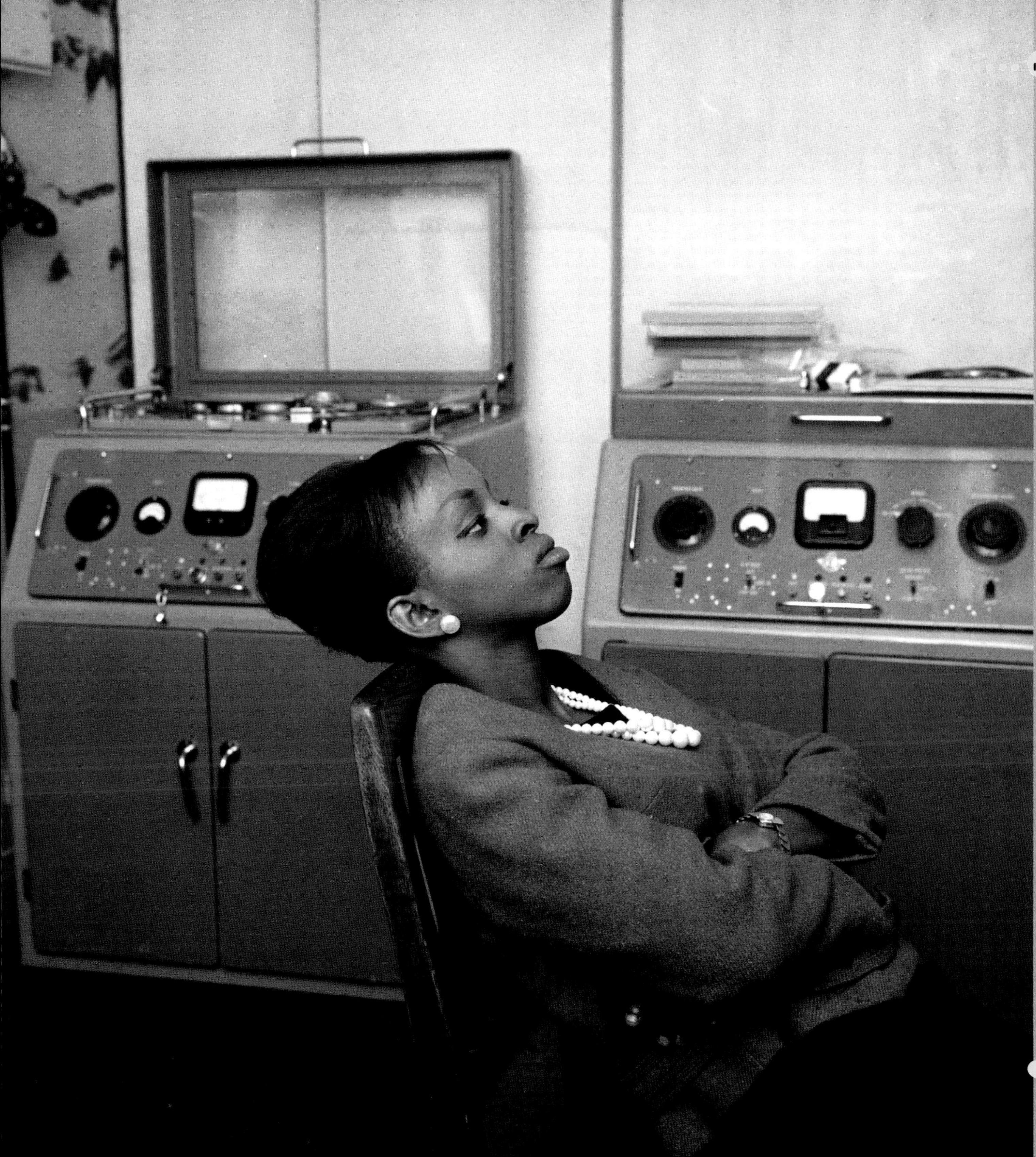

Shortly before The Beatles broke up in 1970, John Lennon began making music with his second wife, Yoko Ono – a Japanese-American pioneering artist and musician. The pair's **Wedding Album**, released in 1969, was their third album of experimental recordings commemorating their recent marriage and included a track originally recorded at Abbey Road in a typical all-night session.

That same year they formed The Plastic Ono Band – a supergroup that enabled them to release a solo album each with the same group of collaborators. These individual albums were also partially recorded at the Studios, but because of their avant-garde nature did not repeat the critical or commercial success of The Beatles.

Lennon's practice of splitting recording sessions between Abbey Road and his home studio was not popular with the Abbey Road staff, despite Lennon's talent and status. "In 1970 I'd already put my name down for Pink Floyd's **Meddle** sessions when Phil McDonald came up to me and said 'Hey, do you want to come down to John and Yoko's house in Ascot? If you won't come with me, I'll have to do it myself because no one else wants to go'," says John Leckie. The album in question ended up being Lennon's 1971 return to traditional songwriting, **Imagine**. Today it is regarded as a modern classic, and the defining moment of Lennon's solo career.

Opposite: *John Lennon and Yoko Ono lie on the floor in Abbey Road Studios. The clouds were later added to the shot by photographer David Nutter. Originally the photo was published upside down, so the pair appeared to be hovering in the sky.*

"Talkin' in our beds for a week
the newspeople said,
'Say, whatcha doin' in bed?'
I said, 'We're only tryin'
to get us some peace"

The Ballad of John and Yoko, 1969

Formative years for Floyd

As the inevitable decline of Merseybeat and the British Invasion beckoned, one band became synonymous with EMI's drive to discover fresh talent and not have its roster swept away by the changing tides of pop music.

Originally a British R&B band formed by student friends Roger Waters, Nick Mason, Richard Wright, and Syd Barrett in 1965, Pink Floyd quickly embraced the psychedelic culture of the 1960s, which inspired improvisation and longer songs than had been the norm. The band also embraced the Studios' multi-track recording technology, which had now become standard.

Also in 1965, Norman Smith was promoted to head of the Parlophone label – after George Martin left the company to set up a new studio as Associated Independent Recording (AIR), although he continued to work at Abbey Road Studios on a freelance basis. Smith signed Pink Floyd in 1967 and produced their debut album, **The Piper at the Gates of Dawn**, at Abbey Road. The nature of the band's initial record deal gave them time to take full advantage of the Studios' facilities and experiment with their output.

Entering the UK chart at No. 6 on release, **The Piper at the Gates of Dawn** is today still credited as one of the seminal albums that ushered in the psychedelic rock movement, altering the pop landscape of the 1970s. Unfortunately, frontman Syd Barrett – the band's main songwriter – frequently clashed with Norman Smith, whose authoritarian style was at odds with Syd's more freeform sensibilities, which didn't always fit the rigid pop mould.

"The black and green scarecrow is sadder than me, But now he's resigned to his fate, 'Cause life's not unkind – he doesn't mind. He stood in a field where barley grows."

The Scarecrow, The Piper at the Gates of Dawn, Syd Barrett, 1967
Published by Westminster Music Ltd. (North America: TRO-Hampshire House Publishing Corp.)

Above: *Syd Barrett in portrait, circa 1968*
Opposite: *Richard Wright, David Gilmour, Roger Waters, and Nick Mason*

The Syd Barrett split

Following the release of **The Piper at the Gates of Dawn**, Barrett's increasingly erratic behaviour prompted the addition of guitarist and vocalist David Gilmour in early 1968. Barrett's revised role as non-performing songwriter proved unworkable, and he quit the band shortly afterwards. Pink Floyd's fresh line-up returned to Abbey Road to complete recording their new album, 1968's **A Saucerful of Secrets** – once again with Norman Smith, who was growing increasingly frustrated at the band's desire to record ever longer songs. Marking a transitional period for Pink Floyd, this was still rock music with underground appeal, illustrated by the album's chart debut at No. 9 in the UK, while all 3 singles released that year made no impact.

Soundtrack success

Alongside work on their own albums, Pink Floyd also ventured into composing soundtracks for movies. Their score for the 1968 British noir film **The Committee** preceded the 1969 issue of their **Soundtrack from the Film More**. Self-produced, this was recorded without Norman Smith and away from Abbey Road, at London's Pye Studios in Marble Arch. The soundtrack again hit the Top Ten and the band's growing fan-base flocked to witness their expansive live show. Pink Floyd was hitting the mainstream. A double album, **Ummagumma**, came next, in November 1969. With extracts from two live sets on one disc, produced by the band, the other disc featured a solo piece from each band member, recorded at Abbey Road, and once more produced by Norman Smith. The stage was set for the band's wholehearted return to Abbey Road, and a success that would rock the world – including the band's first US chart placing, alongside their UK Top Five entry.

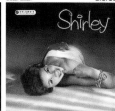

Above and left:

*A diverse selection
of album and single
releases from
the 1960s*

As EMI's roster expanded over the 1960s, it eventually included artists who spanned the realm of popular culture. Pop music continued to provide the soundtrack to other forms of entertainment, and the Studios still recorded comedy and other spoken word performances. American singer, actor, and cabaret star Eartha Kitt exemplified Abbey Road's continued attraction of established international stars. Homegrown British quartet The Swinging Blue Jeans were one of the Merseyside number that debuted in 1963. Their biggest hit was a cover of 1950s rock and roll pioneer Chan Romero's **Hippy Hippy Shake** on the HMV label, which charted at No. 2. A rare live recording of the song by The Beatles also exists.

More famous names

Other artists recording during the same period included Canadian bluesman Long John Baldry, South African balladeer Danny Williams, and comedy poets McGough & McGear. Mike McGear was the stage name of Paul McCartney's brother Mike, who did not wish to trade on his brother's success. His work alongside Roger McGough started when the pair formed the group Scaffold with the entertainer John Gorman. McGear later abandoned poetry and performance for a career in photography and other pursuits.

Other disparate artists of note were the British pop pianist Russ Conway, and American singer, songwriter, and actor P.J. Proby – who moved to London to record in the early 1960s and enlisted the services of Jimmy Page, later lead guitarist of Led Zeppelin – as well as recording **That Means a Lot** – an offcut from the Beatles' **Help!** soundtrack.

How progressive rock,
pop, and comedy

The 1970s and concept albums

defined a decade of change

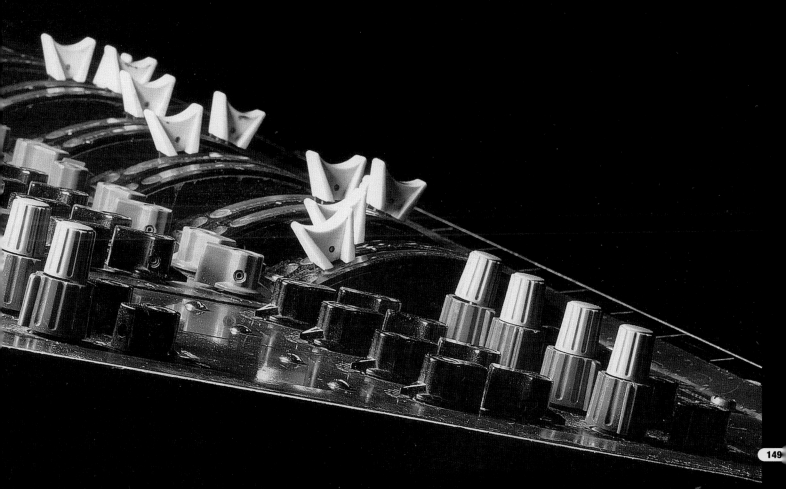

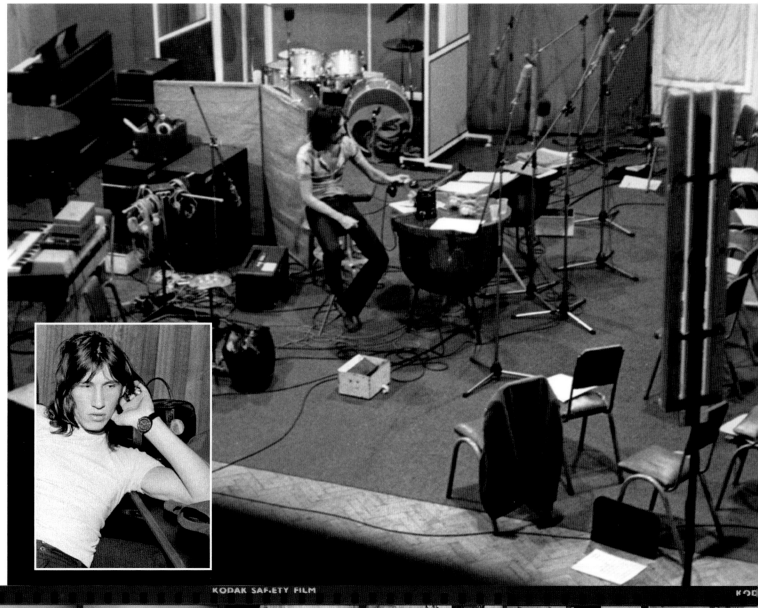

KODAK SAFETY FILM

The 1970s
Era of the album

n 1969, EMI created Harvest Records as an offshoot of Parlophone in order to promote the new breed of progressive rock bands it was signing. Pink Floyd was its greatest success story, as the band eschewed UK singles releases (until 1979) and concentrated on releasing albums that charted highly and sold well. "I took any opportunity to work with Pink Floyd," says John Leckie, who started at Abbey Road as a tape operator in 1970, and who is now one of the world's most renowned music producers. "I also worked with Syd Barrett on his solo material and The Pretty Things – it was all top-notch psychedelic music."

Opposite: *(main) Recording* ***Atom Heart Mother****, 1970, with Nick Mason on drums; (inset) Roger Waters at the mixing desk; (bottom) The band in the Studio 2 control room* **Below:** *(top) David Gilmour; (bottom) Richard Wright*

Multi-track expansion

The first Pink Floyd album to debut at No. 1 in Britain was 1970's ***Atom Heart Mother***, recorded entirely at Abbey Road. It failed to chart highly in the US because of poor publicity, but its critical reception there and in the UK helped secure a host of international tour dates. The album was recorded on eight-track 1" tape and mixed to stereo for the 1970 release. In 1972 it was re-recorded using an eight-track tape machine and mixed in quadraphonic sound – a four-channel playback system acknowledged today as an early version of surround sound.

1971's highly experimental ***Meddle*** continued to build on the band's success with a No. 3 chart debut in the UK, and eventually double-platinum certification in the USA. Ultimately, Abbey Road's facilities could not meet all of the group's technical demands, so some recording took place at other venues with the latest sixteen-track recorders while Abbey Road's equipment was updated.

The Dark Side of the Moon

The band's next foray into Abbey Road was for their mould-breaking **Dark Side of the Moon** opus in 1973. By this time, the Studios had invested in a sixteen-track tape machine which, along with tape loops, formed the backbone of the technological innovations used to record the album. In fact, 16 tracks still proved too few in places – which called for the band to use second-generation copies of a complete recording on one track in order to create more space to add further instrumentation and effects. Abbey Road appointed staff engineer Alan Parsons to work on the album, which was recorded in several sessions between May 1972 and February 1973, while simultaneously being performed as a live piece, debuting in Brighton, UK, in January 1972. The album was a huge success upon its release, selling millions of copies around the world, and has since proved to be one of the top-selling albums of all time. The album propelled the band into the highest echelons of rock status, where they remain.

*Pink Floyd perform **The Dark Side of the Moon** live on one of their many sell-out tour dates*

Pink Floyd's experimentation with different sounds in the Studios, such as the use of a cash register and coins on **Money** (a hit single outside the UK), inspired the band to attempt a new concept album – **Household Objects.** Composed with no conventional musical instruments, the laborious task of converting household objects to supply the requisite effects proved too time-consuming and impractical, and the project, encapsulating two months' work at Abbey Road, was eventually abandoned, its techniques presaging, many years in advance, the modern practice of sampling.

Postcard from the edge

Pink Floyd's last album recorded at Abbey Road was 1975's **Wish You Were Here**. By this point, Alan Parsons had launched his own music career with The Alan Parsons Project. He was replaced by non-EMI engineer Brian Humphries, who had worked on the band's film recordings for **More** and **Zabriskie Point** in 1969. On top of the creative hangover from **The Dark Side of the Moon**, sessions were initially delayed by teething problems with the Abbey Road set-up, but hit their stride once the band refined their direction, producing one of Pink Floyd's most-loved and enduring works. One poignant day, the band were visited at the Studios by Syd Barrett, whose mental deterioration and changed appearance initially made him unrecognizable. Roger Waters – his friend since childhood – later admitted to having wept at his shocking transformation. The album, containing **Shine On You Crazy Diamond**, a song inspired by Barrett, was a huge International success, though, entering the British album charts at No. 1, and going on to top many other charts worldwide, including the US.

Clockwise, from above: *Richard Wright; David Gilmour; cover art for* **Meddle***;*
Atom Heart Mother's cover art; Nick Mason;* **The Dark Side of the Moon***'s cover art; David*
Gilmour; Roger Waters; Nick Mason; Roger Waters; **Wish You Were Here** *cover; Richard Wright*

Opposite: *Arthur Lowe,*
who played Captain George
Mainwaring in **Dad's Army**,
in Control room 1 at Abbey
Road, October 1972
Above, from left:
The **Dad's Army** *cast*
in costume; Arthur Lowe
in his 'civvies'

Comedy remained a strong part of Abbey Road's output during the 1970s, including recordings by the cast of the award-winning BBC sitcom **Dad's Army**, which followed the misadventures of a branch of the Home Guard during the Second World War.

A long-running TV and radio series, with accompanying stage revue, **Dad's Army** also became a feature film in 1971. This brought the cast to Abbey Road – as EMI opted to release a single to coincide with the film's release.

Released by Columbia, **The Dad's Army March** is a version of a composition from the film with added lyrics by The Dad's Army Choir – its main cast members performing in character. The B-side, **What Did You Do in the War?**, was a new recording by the same group. This featured in the **Dad's Army** film only as an instrumental piece, and is notable as it contains a writer's credit for Clive Dunn – one of the programme's stars. Dunn had been an EMI recording artist from 1970, when he recorded his first and best-known single, **Grandad**, which topped the charts in January the following year after a strike at EMI's pressing plant had arguably denied it the chance to be a Christmas No. 1.

In 1972, Columbia issued another single that featured two recordings by the cast. **We Stood Alone** again had the cast perform in character, singing in chorus to another marching-band beat with interjections from the series' familiar voices. Its B-side, **Down Our Way**, is an anachronistic recording about life in modern England in the early 1970s, seen as a tribute to the characters of the fictional Walmington-on-Sea's Home Guard.

"Aeroplanes tied up with string flying, Telephones and talking things sighing,
A radio and phonograph, Charlie Chaplin made us laugh."

Grandad, **Clive Dunn, 1971**

Miss Bette Davis sings

One of the more unusual albums recorded at the Studios in the 1970s was Hollywood actress Bette Davis' only album. Davis began her career in the 1930s, and quickly won acclaim for a series of gritty, confrontational performances in dramas such as *Dangerous* and *Jezebel*, for which she won the Academy Award for Best Actress in 1935 and 1938, respectively. The first woman to do so, she was nominated ten times in total over the course of a career that continued into the 1980s.

Released in 1976, *Miss Bette Davis* – entitled *Miss Bette Davis Sings!* in the United States – was an opportunity for the then 67-year-old actor to record a collection of songs she had previously performed on screen and stage, famous dialogue from her films, and a number of new compositions. Davis was invited to record the album by producer Norman Newell and Roger Webb, who conducted and arranged the music.

Not noted by many as a singer, the album became infamous for exposing Davis' limited vocal range, despite the best efforts of her collaborators to tailor the material to her delivery. It was subsequently deleted and remained unavailable for many years before being reissued in 2003. Today it enjoys a reputation as a curio and collector's item, regarded widely as an ignominious but entertaining misstep.

Clockwise, from left: *Bette Davis sings at Abbey Road; Two shots of the actor at work in Studio 2; The album's inlay; The front cover of* **Miss Bette Davis**; *The back cover of a tape box from the* **Miss Bette Davis** *recording session*

Pilot play on and Ashkenazy appears

The transition period of the 1970s was marked by both classical and pop recordings at Abbey Road. Scottish pop-rock band Pilot was formed by David Paton and Billy Lyall – ex-members of the Bay City Rollers. Alan Parsons acted as producer on Pilot's million-selling single, 1974's **Magic**, and their No. 1, **January**, of 1975. The band made several albums in the 70s, but the line-up gradually dissipated. All four original members, however, collaborated with prog rock duo The Alan Parsons Project (Alan Parsons and Scottish songwriter and composer Eric Woolfson). Deep Purple – early proponents of heavy metal – recorded segments of their breakthrough album **Deep Purple in Rock** at the Studios, issued on the new EMI Harvest label in 1970.

Meanwhile, Russian conductor and pianist Vladimir Ashkenazy began recording at the Studios. Ashkenazy relocated from the USSR to London in 1963, and from there to Iceland with his Icelandic wife in 1968 – taking citizenship there four years later to gain the right to travel. Renowned for his interpretations of Mozart, Russian, and Romantic music, Ashkenazy turned increasingly to conducting. At Abbey Road, he recorded with Israeli violinist Itzhak Perlman, the Philharmonia Orchestra, and many others.

Opposite: *(main) Pilot record in Studio 2; (inset, top) Stuart Tosh; (inset, bottom) David Paton*
Left: *Vladimir Ashkenazy plays the piano at Abbey Road*
Above: ***Deep Purple in Rock*** *cover art and label*

The times they are a-changin'

The 1970s finished as they had begun, with a new and typically diverse wave of music at Abbey Road.

Easy-listening crooner and light entertainer Des O'Connor made many recordings, despite being unhappy with the parking situation at the studios. Other relationships included those with Roy Harper – the guitarist and vocalist whose work included guest vocals on Pink Floyd's *Have a Cigar* – and a young Elton John. Yehudi Menuhin continued crossover collaborations with artists such as jazz violinist Stéphane Grappelli.

Other pop contributors included British psychedelic staple Kevin Ayers, future superstar Kate Bush, and Steve Harley with his band Cockney Rebel. Supporting Harley on one recording was EMI-signed cult star Marc Bolan (of the band T. Rex), whose career ended prematurely in a fatal car crash. British punks The Buzzcocks recorded several demos at the Studios in 1977 before signing to United Artists, which was absorbed by EMI in 1980.

Actors continued to sing, too. A cover of the Bob Dylan song *If Not For You* had provided Olivia Newton-John with her first hit single in 1971, and she signed to EMI in 1974, recording at Abbey Road throughout the decade. British icon Diana Dors featured in 1977, when she recorded *Passing By* – one of several singles released across various labels towards the end of her career.

Clockwise, from top left: *A selection of artists who recorded at Abbey Road in the 70s: Des O'Connor; Roy Harper; Elton John; Stéphane Grappelli and Yehudi Menuhin; Kevin Ayers; Steve Harley; The Buzzcocks; Olivia Newton-John; Diana Dors*

How the Studios took action
to reflect and refocus

Enter film scores and musicals

in the face of hot competition

The 1980s
Comebacks and new artists

During the 1980s, it became necessary for Abbey Road to reflect and refocus. The proliferation of other recording studios throughout the world increased competition, while EMI's merger with Thorn Electrical in 1979 now required the Studios to become a profit centre for the business.

Amidst these new economic pressures, artists continued to record. Anglo-American folk rock duo America had previously been produced by George Martin, although not at Abbey Road. The band first entered the Studios in 1982 to record part of their album **View from the Ground.** It revived their fortunes and the band returned again a year later to record its follow-up, **Your Move**. The sessions made the most of the Studios' space and location, recording the single **The Border** in collaboration with the Royal Philharmonic Orchestra.

One of the most successful British artists to top the charts with recordings from Abbey Road during the 1980s was Kate Bush. The singer-songwriter's third album, 1980's **Never for Ever**, was the first by a British female solo artist to top the UK album charts – and the first by a female artist to debut at No. 1. Like The Beatles, Bush became famous for not just recording in the Studios but writing and experimenting there, too.

"Being on your own in Studio 2 is a fascinating experience," she told the authors of the 2002 book **Abbey Road**. "I felt like there were at least ten other people there with me... I think it's a combination of all the people who have performed there over the years and their combined creativity."

Above: *America in the control room creating* **View from the Ground**
Right: *Kate Bush in Studio 2's control room at a Mark IV desk.*

Time changes the musical

One of the most high-concept musical soundtracks to be recorded at Abbey Road was *Time* – the 1986 West End production of which prompted an all-star album of the same name. A science-fiction tale, with mass-appeal in mind, *Time* follows the adventures of Chris Wilder – a rock musician who is transported into the future to find that he must save the planet. The stage production starred a familiar face within Abbey Road – evergreen pop star Cliff Richard.

The album also featured legendary British actor Laurence Olivier, who was narrator of the stage show, alongside pop icons including Stevie Wonder, Freddie Mercury, Dionne Warwick, and Leo Sayer.

Opposite: *(main) Freddie Mercury, who performed on the* **Time** *album, photographed live in concert with his band Queen; (inset, left) Cliff Richard with Dave Clark – lyricist for* **Time***, formerly of the Dave Clark Five. By the 1980s, he had become a successful director and producer; (inset, right) Cliff Richard performs in the West End*

Left and below, left: *Another* **Time** *performer, singer Stevie Wonder, performs impromptu in Studio 2 at a launch for his album* **Hotter Than July** *in 1980*

Below, right: *Dave Clark with Laurence Olivier*

More pop from Abbey Road

British duo Pet Shop Boys and Swedish trio a-ha were
two examples of the new wave of electronic pop nurtured
at Abbey Road and dominating 1980s' charts. Norwich
natives The Farmer's Boys, however, updated the
clean-cut sound of the 1960s with hints of psychedelic
kitsch. American folk star Art Garfunkel also featured,
as did British actor and singer Michael Crawford –
who recorded hits from his roles in musicals, such as
Phantom of the Opera. Fewer guitar bands featured,
although post-punks Gang of Four from Leeds did record
1981's *Solid Gold* at the Studios. "They said it was like
a gentleman's club and it didn't suit them," remembers
former technician and then Head of Post-Production
Chris Buchanan, "so I suppose it wasn't for everybody!"

Opposite, clockwise from top left: *Art Garfunkel; Duran Duran;
a-ha; Michael Crawford; Pet Shop Boys;*
Above, from left: *Gang of Four's **Solid Gold** sleeve and album
cover; The Farmer's Boys' **Get Out and Walk** album*
Right: *The Farmer's Boys on the steps of Abbey Road*

Lyricist and composer Lionel Bart returned to Abbey Road in 1989 to perform *Happy Endings* – a one-minute jingle for an advertising campaign for the Abbey National Building Society. Filmed at the Studios, the advert featured Bart singing at the piano accompanied by a children's chorus –with strong overtones of his 1960s' hit musical *Oliver!* The success of the piece rekindled Bart's career as he went on to re-write *Oliver!* for its successful West End revival in 1994, under producer Cameron Mackintosh.

Andy Williams sings the classics

Visiting Abbey Road in the 1980s – for the first time – was American easy-listening star Andy Williams. Recording on the US label Columbia from 1962 until 1980, Williams was now approached by songwriters and producers Nicky Graham and Tony Hiller to perform *Greatest Love Classics* with the Royal Philharmonic Orchestra in Studio 1, with some material recorded at CBS Studios in the USA. Classical artists at Abbey Road had pushed boundaries since Yehudi Menuhin collaborated with noted Indian musician Ravi Shankar in the 1960s, but this was the first time the popular singer had attempted to sing melodies based on classical works.

Williams, a long-time fan of classical music, embraced the opportunity and despite the album's unusual nature, it was a success – certified Silver in the United Kingdom with sales of 60,000 copies.

Opposite: *Lionel Bart poses with his junior co-stars at the filming of the Abbey National **Happy Endings** advertising jingle*
Left: *Andy Williams records his **Greatest Love Classics** album with the Royal Philharmonic Orchestra; Andy Williams with musician Herbie Flowers*

Classical stars continue to shine

Among the artists who drove classical recordings to evolve inside Abbey Road was British violin prodigy Nigel Kennedy. A non-conformist, his shared love for jazz and classical music, and a determination to explore and express both passions, led to an eclectic and highly successful career. He began recording in 1984 releasing one jazz and one classical album with Chandos Records, before the first album for his long-term signing to EMI – *Elgar: Violin Concerto in B minor, Op. 61*. This initial performance with the London Philharmonic Orchestra began a collaboration that lasted well into the 1990s.

Kennedy released one other jazz album in the 1980s: *Let Loose* from 1987, in tandem with keyboard player Dave Heath. Other releases celebrated classical composers such as Bartók, Tchaikovsky, Beethoven, and Sibelius. In 1989, his version of Vivaldi's *The Four Seasons* with the English Chamber Orchestra – also recorded at the Studios – sold more than two million copies and confirmed Kennedy as a crossover star.

Ousset's master class

A French pianist with similar child star credentials to Kennedy, Cécile Ousset signed to EMI in 1982 and delivered a remarkable series of recordings over the next two decades. Her first recording for HMV brought together concertos by Liszt and Saint-Saëns. Best known for her interpretations of French composers, Ousset's body of work spanned the classical genre as she collaborated with the London Symphony Orchestra, conductor Simon Rattle, and others. In 1982, she made her first solo recording for HMV – pairing Mussorgsky's *Pictures at an Exhibition* with Ravel's *Gaspard de la Nuit*. Ousset formalized her in-demand masterclasses as an annual event held in her home village of Puycelsi in south-west France from 1984, but continued to record at Abbey Road into the 1990s.

Opposite, clockwise from top left: *Kennedy plays the violin, December 1987; Kennedy with conductor Jeffrey Tate; Cécile Ousset with conductor Sir Neville Marriner; Cécile Ousset recording in July 1984*

Abbey Road goes to the movies

The 1980s saw a significant development, with the strategic expansion of the recording of film scores. A Ken Townsend initiative, Anvil-Abbey Road Screen Sound was formed between the Studios and Anvil Post Production, which in 1980 was about to lose its sound stage.

"Abbey Road supplied not only the space but the recording equipment and technical backup as well as handling bookings," says Townsend. "They supplied the rest of the staff and the projectors. The work started flowing in like nothing on Earth."

"I think if Studio 1 had been divided up into a number of smaller recording and mixing spaces, which was prevalent elsewhere at the time, I'm not sure Abbey Road would still be going today" says Simon Campbell, Head of Technical Services, referring to an idea to boost revenue prior to the new venture. "A lot of people were in favour of that idea," adds Townsend, "but I stuck to my guns and after six months it proved a huge success."

The Studios strike back

Among the first Hollywood blockbusters to record scores at Abbey Road were the second and third parts of the original *Star Wars* trilogy – *The Empire Strikes Back* and *Return of the Jedi*, in 1980 and 1983 respectively. American conductor John Williams and the London Symphony Orchestra worked together on both occasions, reprising their roles from the first film at the start of their many collaborations at Abbey Road.

Opposite: *The London Symphony Orchestra pauses during recording one of the **Star Wars** scores in Studio 1, with conductor John Williams and the movie's writer and director George Lucas*
Inset: *Darth Vader – the iconic villain of the original **Star Wars** trilogy*

Lights, cameras, and more action

John Williams and the London Symphony Orchestra had also worked together at Abbey Road in 1981 on **Raiders of the Lost Ark** – a Steven Spielberg production and the first movie completely scored at the Studios.

Classical work was dropping alarmingly due to a downturn in vinyl sales. Decca, EMI's biggest rival, closed and EMI was lagging behind in the adoption of CDs, all of which impacted on classical recording budgets. "The classical division producers who used Studio 1 weren't prepared to pay that much money, plus they wanted to book the studio a year in advance for something like three hours," says Townsend, explaining how the balance in studio time noticeably shifted from classical to film projects in this era. The Studios opened up to third party customers and were now required to make a profit

The joint venture between Abbey Road and Anvil Films ended amicably at the end of 1984 but by this time the Studios' reputation and technical capability to accommodate the demands of large film had saved Studio 1 as a single space – and once more promoted it as a desirable venue. "It has fine acoustics so we can capture specific close-up aspects of the orchestra and still get the bloom of the full room itself," John Williams told **The Telegraph** in a 2005 interview.

Opposite: Harrison Ford stars as Indiana Jones in **Raiders of the Lost Ark**, 1981

Insets: An eponymous otherworld creature from **Aliens**, 1986

> So much of what we do is ephemeral and quickly forgotten, even by ourselves, so it's gratifying to have something you have done linger in people's memories.

John Williams

Science fiction and superheroes

Abbey Road continued as a venue for recording film scores throughout the 1980s. In 1985, American conductor and composer Michael Kamen – with a classical pedigree and a background in rock music – arrived to score Terry Gilliam's cult sci-fi and fantasy satire **Brazil**. Although the theme song used in the movie features American singer-songwriter Geoff Muldaur on vocals, Kamen originally recorded a version with Kate Bush.

Another American composer, Danny Elfman scored his friend Tim Burton's 1989 mainstream hit **Batman** at Abbey Road. Elfman was not happy with the final mix, but his instrumental score was a critical and commercial success released alongside the film's soundtrack, written by the American artist Prince.

Costume and historical dramas

In 1985, the Merchant Ivory adaptation of E.M. Forster's classic Edwardian novel **A Room with a View** was scored at the Studios. Composer Richard Robbins worked with the London Philharmonic Orchestra and conductor Sir John Pritchard on a blend of his own compositions and classical pieces by Puccini, reflecting the film's partial Italian setting.

Another hybrid score was that of **The Last Emperor** – Bernardo Bertolucci's 1987 biopic of Pu Yi, the last Emperor of China. The soundtrack featured several pieces recorded at Abbey Road by Japanese composer Ryuichi Sakamoto, who also acted in the film. American songwriter David Byrne and Chinese composer Cong Su also contributed, and the three shared the 1987 Oscar for Best Original Score.

Clockwise, from top left: *Jonathan Pryce stars as government clerk Sam Lowry, transformed in Terry Gilliam's **Brazil** of 1985; Maggie Smith stars as Charlotte Bartlett in **A Room with a View**, 1985; Virtuoso Chinese flautist Guo Yue, who performed on **The Last Emperor**'s prize-winning soundtrack; Peter O'Toole and Wu Tao in **The Last Emperor**, 1987; Michael Keaton as Batman in Tim Burton's caped crusader franchise, 1989*

Miss Bartlett was startled. Generally at a pension people looked them over for a day or two before speaking, and often did not find out that they would 'do' till they had gone. She knew that the intruder was ill-bred, even before she glanced at him.

A Room with a View,
E.M. Forster, 1908

How rock and pop revivals,
award-winning movies, and musicals

Independent
spirit

set the scene for
the renaissance of cool

The 1990s
Settling scores old and new

The number of film scores recorded at Abbey Road increased steadily over the course of the 1990s. At the same time, pop music was being recorded at a multitude of smaller-scale venues – copies of EMI's model, albeit on a reduced scale. Some of these had even been founded by former Abbey Road employees, such as George Martin's AIR. The Studios had effectively become a victim of their own success.

Rival set-ups could not compete, however, with Abbey Road's unique mix of space, expertise, and technology – not to mention its history. The sheer number of seminal artists who had recorded within its walls in the past was enough to continue to attract a number of big names and new artists – all of whom were keen to experience the fabled Abbey Road magic.

Studio 1 was Abbey Road's prize asset, and clients from the movie world vied to book sessions. In 1994, American composer Elliot Goldenthal visited to record part of his score for the highly-anticipated **Interview with the Vampire: The Vampire Chronicles** – the long-awaited film adaptation of Anne Rice's multi million-selling books. Goldenthal composed the score to reflect the gothic, romantic themes of the film in collaboration with its director, Neil Jordan.

"I like the sound at Abbey Road," Goldenthal told **Crescendo & Jazz Music Magazine** in 1997. "I love working with English musicians, especially the strings. They don't play with excessive vibrato. Strings use too much vibrato in the States."

Debussy and Bizet were cited by critics as his chief classical influences. The score also featured contributions from The American Boychoir – an internationally-renowned choral group. A resounding success, the score earned Goldenthal his first Oscar and Golden Globe nominations.

Opposite: *Brad Pitt stars in **Interview with the Vampire: The Vampire Chronicles** as the vampire Louis*
Right: *Tom Cruise's vampire prosthetics for his role as Lestat. The actor insisted on a private set so that shots of the make-up would not leak to the press.*

> I've discovered that I don't have that much talent, really... No matter how many years I work on something I'm never going to get to Beethoven's level.

Elliot Goldenthal, *Crescendo & Jazz Music Magazine,* **1997**

Mel Gibson braves Abbey Road

When Hollywood star Mel Gibson chose *Braveheart* as only his second film to direct, it was clear that he would have a large project on his hands. A three-hour historical epic set in 13th-century Scotland, *Braveheart* took over two years to make and required thousands of extras for its huge battle scenes. Co-produced by his own company, Icon, Gibson agreed to star as the film's protagonist – the warrior William Wallace – in order to secure its $60 million budget. Once the project was underway, it was clear that Gibson was to have a hand in every stage of the process, including its soundtrack.

Multiple successes

Gibson visited Abbey Road in 1995 with US composer, orchestrator, and conductor James Horner and the London Symphony Orchestra to record the film's score. This echoed elements of Rachmaninov's *Symphony No. 1*, and was later to become one of Horner's trademark motifs. His score was among the ten Oscar nominations received by the movie, and its success led to a second release – *More Music from Braveheart* – in 1997. Snippets from Horner's original score were also used for 1995's space exploration saga *Apollo 13* – nominated for Best Original Dramatic Score alongside that of *Braveheart* – as well as for the trailer to the Tom Hanks drama *Cast Away* of 2000.

Left: *Mel Gibson shares a joke from behind the control desk in Studio 1* **Opposite:** *(main) Gibson as William Wallace, in one of the most iconic roles of his career; (insets) Horner conducts the London Symphony Orchestra as they record the score for* **Braveheart**, *which Gibson described on the DVD issue of the movie as "One of the great scores... Horner delivered, big time."*

> Would you be willin' to trade all the days, from this day to that, for one chance, just one chance, to come back here and tell our enemies that they may take our lives, but they'll never take... our freedom!

William Wallace, *Braveheart*

INFINITE SPACE
INFINITE TERROR

THE YEAR IS 2047: A RESCUE
MISSION IS SENT TO THE
OUTER REACHES OF OUR SOLAR
SYSTEM TO SALVAGE THE
EVENT HORIZON,
A PROTOTYPE SPACESHIP
MISSING FOR THE LAST SEVEN
YEARS. AS THE CREW MEMBERS
SEARCH FOR SURVIVORS, THEY
DISCOVER THE TERRIFYING
SECRETS THAT LIE WITHIN THE
MYSTERIOUS SPACESHIP.

EVENT HORIZON

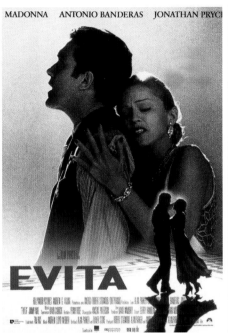

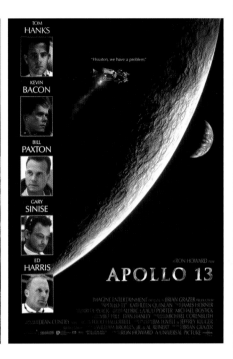

Peace of mind? I have no peace of mind!

I've had no peace of mind since we lost

America. Forests, old as the world itself...

meadows... plains... strange, delicate flowers...

immense solitudes... and all nature new to art...

all ours... Mine. Gone. A paradise... lost.

George III, *The Madness of King George*

Biopics and deep space

If the 1980s established an international flavour in the films scored at Abbey Road, the 1990s made it intergalactic. Deep-space horror **Event Horizon** allowed US composer Michael Kamen to innovate and pair the London Metropolitan Orchestra with British techno-electronica dance music duo Orbital in 1997. The 1998 meteor drama **Deep Impact** was another success for James Horner, who conducted the City of Prague Philharmonic Orchestra – mastering the recording at the Studios.

Back on Planet Earth, 1994's **The Madness of King George** successfully adapted Alan Bennett's play about George III. Its score was a mix of Handel and new pieces by the film's composer, George Fenton. **Evita** told the story of Eva Perón – the first lady of Argentina from 1946 to 1952. Former EMI assistant producer Tim Rice and musical magnate Sir Andrew Lloyd Webber teamed up to repeat the success of their original stage production, from which the 1996 film was adapted.

From left: *Nigel Hawthorne stars as troubled monarch George III; The poster for* **Event Horizon***, a science fiction/ horror cult classic; Madonna and Antonio Banderas as Eva Perón and Che in* **Evita***; The poster for* **Deep Impact***, in which a comet threatens to destroy Earth; The poster for* **Apollo 13***, the dramatic true story of the ill-fated 13th Apollo mission – Annie Lennox's solo vocal performance was recorded at Abbey Road*

Classical music goes pop

The formation of the EMI Classics label in 1990 was a successful attempt to create a single, recognizable brand for the label's classical output and, by extension, much of the classical music recorded at Abbey Road.

The biggest star to feature on the label was British violinist Vanessa-Mae. She had a similar appeal to another unorthodox crossover musician – Nigel Kennedy. Like Kennedy, she upset the norms by looking more like a pop star. Where Kennedy reserved his electric violin for jazz sessions, Vanessa-Mae often chose to play classical pieces on modern instruments – terming her style "violin techno-acoustic fusion".

Making her mark

Recorded in part at Abbey Road, **The Violin Player** of 1995 was the 16-year-old Vanessa-Mae's first album for EMI and her major label debut. For many, the violinist's prodigious talent harked back to the precocity of the Studios' previous young female stars. The album topped the charts on its release, selling over eight million copies, and established Vanessa-Mae as a global star. Her next Abbey Road recordings were sessions for 1997's **Storm** and **China Girl** albums, the scope of which ranged from collaborations with the London Philharmonic Orchestra to **I Feel Love** – a vocal cover of American disco star Donna Summers' 1977 hit.

Opposite: *Vanessa-Mae plays live at the launch of her 1995 album* **The Violin Player**, *which broke down barriers between classical and pop music*

Inset: *Vanessa-Mae poses for a promo shot at the same event*

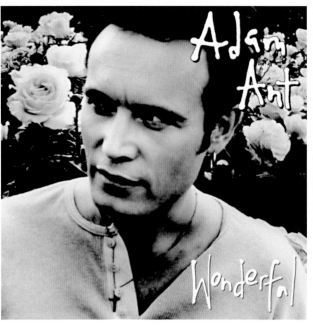

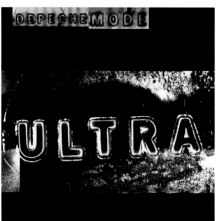

The rebirth of cool

As guitar music came back into fashion in the 1990s, its bands recorded at Abbey Road in greater numbers. Star indie act Radiohead completed recording of their sophomore album ***The Bends*** at the Studios in 1995, mastered in-house by Chris Blair. Acting as producer was former Abbey Road staff member John Leckie – now freelancing and greatly in demand. Radiohead's third album, ***OK Computer***, was also mastered by Blair at Abbey Road – where the string sections were recorded. Issued on Parlophone in 1997, this experimental album achieved multi-platinum status, with great critical and commercial success.

In the early 1980s, Adam Ant had hit the Top Ten several times with his post-punk rock/New Romantic group Adam and the Ants, and as a solo artist. He recorded his 1995 comeback album ***Wonderful*** at Abbey Road, and developed a flourishing acting career.

Depêche Mode, electronic music giants, used Studio facilities to record parts of their ninth album, ***Ultra***, in 1997. A collaboration with producer and DJ Tim Simenon, ***Ultra*** shot to No. 1 in the Albums Chart and achieved Gold status.

Above, from left:
Adam Ant's 1995 album
Wonderful; *Depêche*
*Mode's **Ultra** from 1997*
Opposite: *(main)*
Radiohead frontman
Thom Yorke performs
live at Utrecht in 1997;
(insets, from top)
Radiohead's albums
The Bends *(1995) and*
OK Computer *(1997)*

More indie maestros

Not all the artists who recorded at Abbey Road during guitar rock's resurgence in the 1990s were part of EMI's roster. One of the biggest acts to emerge during this period – Manchester-based rock band Oasis – was signed to the Creation label. Like many of their contemporaries, Oasis recorded and mixed their albums at numerous different studios. Heavily influenced by The Beatles, Oasis referenced the band both lyrically and musically, so it was hardly a surprise that they wanted to record at Abbey Road. The 1996 sessions for their third album, the multi-platinum seller **Be Here Now**, have become legendary for their rowdiness. EMI Classics producer John Fraser quit his session in Studio 1 to storm into Studio 2, demanding that the Mancunian guitar heroes turn down their volume. Abbey Road finally banned the musicians from the building, although they managed to return to the Studios to record their seventh album, **Dig Out Your Soul,** in 2008 – reputedly after paying up-front and in cash.

Paul Weller was another luminary to record at Abbey Road. Despite the fact that he had heavily influenced the course of British guitar music over two decades with The Jam and then with The Style Council, Weller didn't record at the Studios until 1995. The session on that date was remarkable: Weller collaborated with Paul McCartney and Noel Gallagher to record a version of The Beatles' **Come Together** for **The Help Album** – famously recorded and released within a week to raise funds for the War Child charity.

Opposite: *Oasis frontmen Noel and Liam Gallagher, in 1994*
Left: *Paul Weller performing in 1994*

As rock and indie music flourished, alternative rock band from Cardiff, the Manic Street Preachers mixed tracks from their fourth album **Everything Must Go** at the Studios – where the album was also mastered, by Chris Blair, and cut. Released in 1996, this was the cult band's first offering since the disappearance of their member Richey Edwards (Richey James). Also sprinkling Abbey Road's unique essence on their sixth album **Blue** came British soul group Simply Red with lead vocalist Mick Hucknell in 1998.

Blur initially came to Abbey Road in 1995 to re-record **To The End** with Françoise Hardy. Frontman Damon Albarn has continued his relationship with the Studios over many years across his varied collaborations and side projects. He went on to appear in the Studios' **Live from Abbey Road** series as part of the alternative rock venture The Good, The Bad & The Queen in 2006, and used its facilities to master 2010's **The Fall** album by his virtual band Gorillaz.

One noted charity recording at the Studios in the 1990s was Boy George's re-recording of **Karma Chameleon** – his 1983 hit with New Romantic band Culture Club. British Telecom's campaign with homeless charity Message Home gave 100 competition winners the chance to accompany the charismatic British pop star in 1999.

Left: *The Manic Street Preachers performing at The Forum, London, in 1996*
Below, from left: *Lead singer with Blur, Damon Albarn, on stage in 1997 at the height of the 'Britpop' era; Mick Hucknell of Simply Red on stage at Hyde Park in 1999; Boy George sings with Culture Club, who reformed after a 12-year split in 1998*

Abbey Road's musical numbers

In addition to film score work at Abbey Road, the Studios played host to various musical productions as the demand emerged for original cast recordings. In 1991, the Old Vic theatre in London staged a revival of 1943 Broadway musical **Carmen Jones** by American librettist Oscar Hammerstein II – directed by Simon Callow. An updated version of Georges Bizet's 1875 opera **Carmen**, it transposes the original plot of a soldier seduced by the titular character from 1820s Spain to the Second World War era with an all-black cast.

Carmen Jones at Abbey Road

The cast of the 1991 production descended on Studio 1 on 6 June 1991 and recorded for three days. The subsequent recording was praised for re-orchestrating much of Bizet's original score to include modern elements that better fitted its 1940s setting – such as saxophone parts that reflected a jazz influence – whilst retaining the original arias and the material's operatic genus. This fully captured the unique crossover appeal of the ambitious production, which was further recognized with a trio of Olivier awards for Best Director, Best Actress, and Best New Musical in 1992.

Above and right: *The cast of **Carmen Jones** in Studio 1, including Wilhelmenia Fernandez and Damon Evans, Sharon Benson and Michael Austin. The two pairs of actors alternated in the lead parts of Carmen and Joe because of the vocal demands of the show's eight performances a week.*
Top right: *The 2002 re-issue of the cast recording*

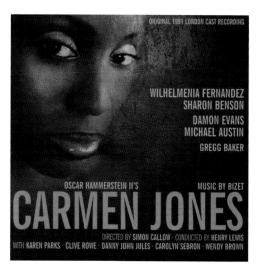

ORIGINAL 1991 LONDON CAST RECORDING

WILHELMENIA FERNANDEZ
SHARON BENSON

DAMON EVANS
MICHAEL AUSTIN

GREGG BAKER

OSCAR HAMMERSTEIN II'S

MUSIC BY BIZET

CARMEN JONES

DIRECTED BY SIMON CALLOW · CONDUCTED BY HENRY LEWIS

WITH KAREN PARKS · CLIVE ROWE · DANNY JOHN JULES · CAROLYN SEBRON · WENDY BROWN

How the digital age
transformed the industry

The Studios' legacy lives on

as Abbey Road went live

Live action and fantasy flicks

irmly in the 21st century, Abbey Road maintains its cutting-edge presence in the music industry. Studio 1 is still the nonpareil venue for recording film scores, and artists flock to record at Abbey Road's elite facilities.

One recent hit is the **Live from Abbey Road** television series, launched in 2006. Featuring performances interspersed with brief to-camera and voice-over interviews, it welcomed back previous visitors to the Studios, as well as new artists keen to experience the magic.

"As with many things, if you turn back then it was The Beatles who came up with the original idea," says the series' creator, Michael Gleason. "They did the very first worldwide broadcast from Abbey Road Studios and it went live to about 350 million people."

Gleason made the first series after meeting musician, producer, and Abbey Road devotee Peter Van Hooke. "He'd carried that idea around for about 12 years but nothing ever happened with it," Gleason says. "So I ended up funding and producing the first series and we've gone from there."

Going global

To book the artists he wanted for the programme, Gleason teamed up with music industry veteran Fraser Kennedy. "We decided to go for all kinds of artists, from jazz to country, and pop," explains Gleason. "It became an international show, featuring international artists, to be sold internationally. Fraser opened his book with 25 to 30 years of relationships with managers and record labels. We'd book the show independently, again, of any record label, any TV company... we did it all by ourselves."

The simple format and Studios' appeal was enough to attract the talent. "We never had any conditions from or had to make any assurances to anybody," says Kennedy. "It was all about being the artist and it was all built around them. That's why they all had their day. They came in at 8am and you went home at 8pm. Everybody got what they wanted."

Clockwise, from top left:

Legendary jazz saxophonist Wayne Shorter; Jazz and classical trumpet player Wynton Marsalis' **Live from Abbey Road** *set in 2006 combined hits and improvisation; Shorter and jazz great Herbie Hancock get organized between takes; singer-songwriter Corinne Bailey Rae accompanies Hancock, with Shorter on saxophone, in 2007*

Artists in control

From the outset, Gleason and Kennedy aimed to give their guests as much creative control as possible over the music they recorded for *Live from Abbey Road*.

"I made it a licensed show," says Gleason. "We made the editorial decisions and that really was helpful because we had real creative control... We could do what we want."

"We give the artist the opportunity to mix the sound, to be involved with the sound," adds Kennedy. "What you find with a lot of TV shows is that they're not like that. Often we'll hear late at night that the bands have heard the whole sound and that they're happy. They go home happy. As a result, the show's reputation has spread right across the world."

Another key reason for the show's success was that its creators pursued the acts they wanted, which took some time in the case of world-touring, million-selling artists.

"It took us two years to get Green Day," says Kennedy. "They couldn't stop talking about how much fun they had," adds Gleason. "They said it was the best TV they'd ever done."

This place is beautiful and has a really special

feel. The Beatles said 'All you need is love'

and I think this place understands that.

Melody Gardot, jazz and blues artist

Time is precious inside the Studios

As sessions for *Live from Abbey Road* got into full swing, studio space was also in demand from other clients. This led to some logistical problems for Fraser Kennedy.

"I'd have six months on hold," says Kennedy. "I used to take a week on, a week off, another week on, week off... right through for six months, and then Colette Barber, the studio manager, and I would negotiate. Every day we would be swapping dates over because I had to have the time when the artists were available."

Occasionally, the programme-makers tried to be innovative with the space, as when Debbie Harry joined the line-up of the show at short notice in 2011.

"Because Studio 2 was booked, we had this idea to film an acoustic set in the Studios' garden. It was all great, but then the rain came down," laughs Kennedy. "It was like a typhoon. We had to bring in the remote-control unit, steal a corner of Studio 2, and do it on the hoof."

Opposite: *(main) Beach Boys legend Brian Wilson in a 2008 session in Studio 2; (inset) Debbie Harry celebrates her birthday with Michael Gleason in Studio 2, while recording for* **Live from Abbey Road** *in 2011*
Right: *(top) Wilson sings in Studio 2; (bottom) The drum kit on Wilson's set*

The record company gets the artists to the front door then we take care of them and give them back at the end of the day. Once they were in the building, they're away from all the chaos. That's what's so great about it.

Fraser Kennedy, Associate Producer *Live from Abbey Road*

Talent show

Together with the unheralded freedom afforded to artists when recording sessions for *Live from Abbey Road*, the building itself often works its magic on guests before they've recorded a note.

"This venue is so special to them," says Gleason. "It's like tennis players playing at Wimbledon. For a musician to play here is the same thing. We had Cee Lo Green on his knees coming up the stairs outside. He's massive as an artist. That's just how they feel when they come in here."

Behind the cameras, *Live from Abbey Road* is a relatively small operation. A staff of six put the show together. "Our team works together very closely," says Gleason. "We have a tight budget and everybody is willing to do everything."

"If someone feels like they can do a job better than everybody else, then we won't work with them, because we won't tolerate that," he adds. "It's not a producer or a director, it's about the artist. That's it."

Above: *British indie rock band Elbow in session in Studio 2 in 2008. Elbow also recorded a live version of their Mercury Prize-winning album **The Seldom Seen Kid** with the BBC Concert Orchestra in Studio 1 in 2009.*
Opposite: *Bat For Lashes – British pop musician Natasha Khan – performs in 2010*

"When we were young, we used to be at our local studios 24 hours a day. I got a job there just so we could have access. Now, I wouldn't say it was nine 'til five – it's probably like midday 'til four..."

Guy Garvey, Elbow

Rare and unusual footage

The unique nature of the *Live from Abbey Road* sessions results in a large amount of variation across its sessions.

British jazz-funk band Jamiroquai filled Studio 2 with 16 band members – a record for the series.

"There were probably about 35 people actually working in the room, so it was tight!" says Kennedy.

British trip-hop pioneers Massive Attack and Irish singer-songwriter Damien Rice were among those who made exceptions to their rules.

"It's the only TV Massive Attack have done and they don't do interviews," says Kennedy. "Well, we couldn't stop them talking. It's a funny thing, there's a disarming process that takes place when people come in here."

Damien Rice experienced a similar phenomenon.

"The record company said 'He doesn't want to do an interview'," says Kennedy. "We got talking to him and asked why, and he said 'I'm fed up of talking about myself,' and then carried on talking."

Finally, it turns out, the series may never have happened if Kennedy had got the engineer's job he applied for at Abbey Road 40 years ago.

"Someone missed out somewhere," he smiles, "Maybe it was me!"

Clockwise, from top left: *Live From Abbey Road* performances:
David Gilmour; Jay Kay; Damien Rice; Def Leppard; Corinne Bailey Rae

More gold for the silver screen

Entering the 21st century added more big names to the films scored at Abbey Road. Music for all three instalments of director Peter Jackson's **Lord of the Rings** trilogy were produced at the Studios, and first screened between 2001 and 2003.

Most of the music was recorded at The Watford Colosseum. Abbey Road engineers then mixed the recordings in the Penthouse Studio after editing its various suites.

On one occasion, the film was being mixed right up until the day the print master was about to be created. "For the second film, I worked 86 days without a day off, doing roughly 12-hour days," says Mirek Stiles. "Everything about those films was epic." The music recording process for the trilogy was extensively documented in the bonus material on the Extended Edition DVDs, which give a fascinating look behind the scenes.

Above: *The boys of the London Oratory School Schola record for the* **Lord of the Rings** *score, and take a break in the Abbey Road Studios' canteen*
Opposite: *Icelandic indie pop singer Emiliana Torrini records* **Gollum's Song**. *Torrini replaced fellow Icelandic singer Björk when the latter fell pregnant.*

From the ashes a fire shall be woken,
A light from the shadows shall spring;
Renewed shall be blade that was broken,
The crownless again shall be king.

The Song of Aragorn,
The Fellowship of the Ring

Return of the kingmakers

Abbey Road continued to operate as a base for the **Lord of the Rings** franchise partly because of its excellent telecommunication facilities – essential during regular visits from the films' director, New Zealander Peter Jackson, and composer, Canadian Howard Shore, who each netted their first Academy Awards for their efforts.

State-of-the-art video-conferencing had in fact been pioneered at Abbey Road Studios during work with American producer and director George Lucas on the second film in the original **Star Wars** trilogy – **The Empire Strikes Back**, released in 1980.

"George Lucas wanted to be able to speak to his people back at Skywalker Ranch [Lucas's Californian home] while he was working on the music," says IT and communications manager Jim Jones. "He paid for a satellite link back to his office so he could see the dailies. It was fascinating to see the way he worked, the detail of what he got them to change."

215

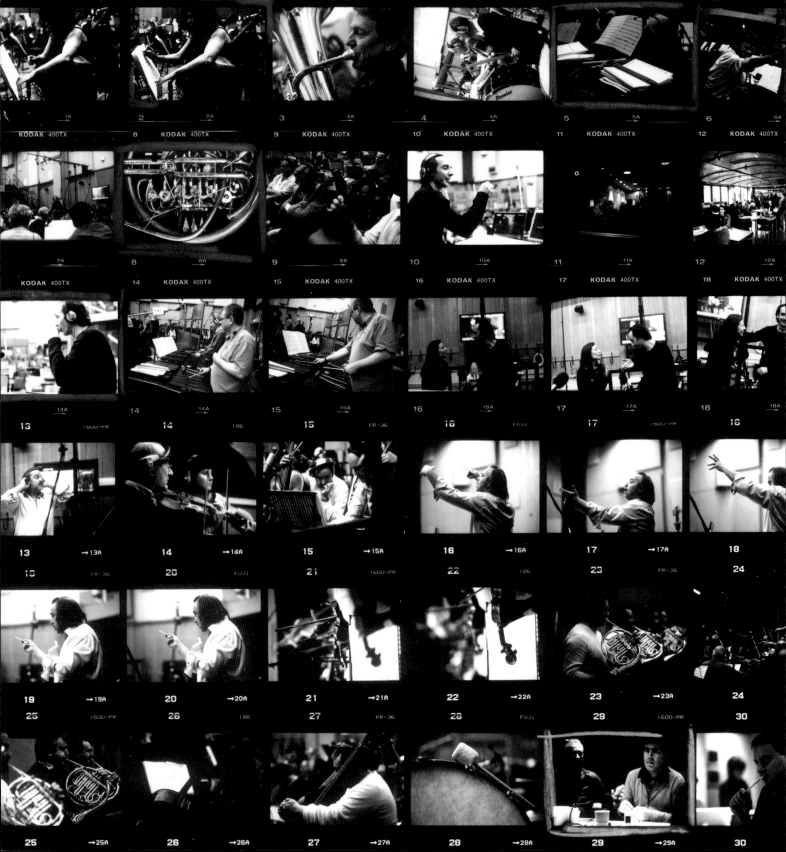

Family favourites at Abbey Road

Another successful franchise of fantasy adaptations to feature at Abbey Road in the 2000s was the *Chronicles of Narnia* series. British composer Harry Gregson-Williams part-recorded the score for the first film – *The Lion, the Witch and the Wardrobe* – at the Studios. Elements of the soundtrack for the second, *Prince Caspian*, were mixed by Peter Cobbin at Abbey Road, while David Arnold – composer of *Voyage of the Dawn Treader*, the third film – also recorded strings there. The soundtracks were an unusual mix of orchestral and choral pieces, along with other genres such as ancient folk and recordings by modern artists. The first soundtrack of the series achieved a Golden Globe nomination.

In 2007, the acclaimed *Golden Compass* score composed by Alexandre Desplat was part-recorded at the Studios, and also mixed and mastered there. Award-winning Spanish composer Javier Navarrete recorded his score for the fantasy film *Inkheart* – an adaptation of a bestselling children's book – at the Studios and between 2002 and 2011 Abbey Road recorded soundtracks for several of the record-breaking *Harry Potter* franchise, working with composers John Williams, Nicholas Hooper, and Alexandre Desplat.

Left: *Studio 1 during a break from scoring* **Harry Potter and the Order of the Phoenix**
Above: *Film stills from* **The Golden Compass** *(left),* **Inkheart** *(centre), and on the set of* **Harry Potter** *(right)*
Opposite: *(top) Contact sheets show recording sessions for* **The Golden Compass** *with composer Alexandre Desplat; (bottom)* **Inkheart** *sessions with Javier Navarrete and Abbey Road engineer Andrew Dudman*

Adventures in sound

Abbey Road has a healthy working relationship with Hollywood, far beyond its links with fantasy franchises. Warner Bros. and DreamWorks number among the major production companies to favour the Studios for their films, which include the latter's *Shrek* of 2001. For many, Abbey Road is the venue of choice for soundtrack recording. Sunny Park, Executive in Charge of Music for Dreamworks Animation notes, "Every recording experience I've had at Abbey Road has been perfect. What I love most is how welcoming they are."

Classical artists frequently record film scores as part of their affiliation with prestigious orchestras. As a solo artist, and a principal cellist for the London Metropolitan Orchestra and the English Chamber Orchestra, British cellist Caroline Dale spans the genres of pop, classical, film, and computer games – the most recent addition to Abbey Road's repertoire. Her film work at Abbey Road includes 2010 British drama *The Kid*, adapted from the Kevin Davis autobiography, while she also performed on the soundtrack to computer game *Motorstorm Apocalypse* – on both occasions with the London Metropolitan Orchestra. Her collaborations in the pop world include those with Jimmy Page and Robert Plant, U2, Oasis, and David Gilmour.

> Growing up and dreaming of the recording music career that I might have, Abbey Road Studios was the "Shangri La", the gold standard, the pinnacle. Getting to work at Abbey Road years later on *The Lord of the Rings* series, the *Harry Potter* series, and so much, much more, has been that dream come true. The continued commitment by Abbey Road to represent all things excellent in the recording arts has made it hard to consider any venue better for film soundtrack recording.

Paul Broucek, President of Music, Warner Brothers Pictures

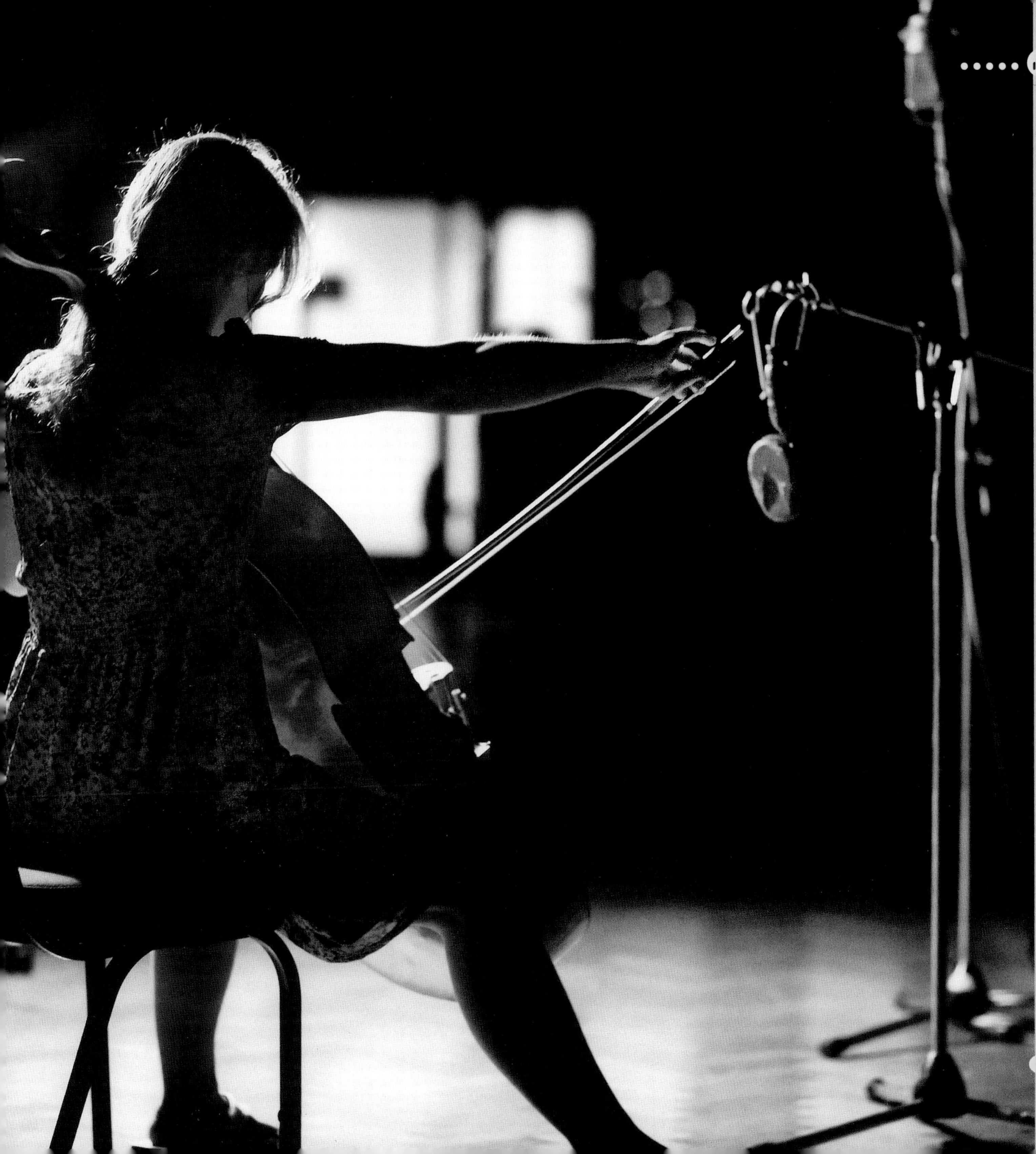

Left: *David Burt, Steve Balsamo,
and Juliet Caton as Reverend
Rufus Griswold, Poe, and Virginia*
Above, left: *Poe and Virginia embrace*
Above, right: *John Otway and his
choir of 300-plus voices record*
The House of the Rising Sun
Opposite: *American singer-songwriter
Regina Spektor visits Studio 2 to
perform* **The Call** *for* **Prince Caspian**

In addition to its film-score work in the 2000s, the Studios also hosted a live musical
in 2003. The world premiere of **Poe**, based on the life and works of American author
Edgar Allan Poe, took place in Studio 1. Brainchild of the late Eric Woolfson, co-founder
of prog-rock supergroup The Alan Parsons Project, **Poe**'s soundtrack was recorded for
commercial release, alongside a DVD. The show ran for over 18 months at the
Halle Opera House in Germany.

Indie and anti-folk

On the indie front, British singer-songwriter and self-styled underdog John Otway broke
the record for bringing most people to record at the Studios – 1000 fans, split over three
sessions, to sing backing vocals for his cover of the American folk song **The House of
the Rising Sun**. The B-side to his single **Bunsen Burner – The Hit Mix**, it entered the UK
Singles Chart at No. 9 on 6 October 2002.

Hailing from the anti-folk scene in New York City, Russian-born singer-songwriter and
pianist Regina Spektor also came to Abbey Road, to record her song **The Call for Narnia**
from blockbuster **Prince Caspian** in 2008.

How the Studios create an ambience,
enticing and inspiring artists

Behind
closed doors

to step inside and stay

Inside the Studios
The largest room

tudio 1 – Abbey Road's largest recording space – was the scene of its inaugural performance in 1931 by Sir Edward Elgar. A bright and airy room, its high ceiling and pale blue décor now lend it a vast, open feel – rather different from the darker art deco design of its early days, which even featured a stage at one end. As with all the recording suites, Studio 1 has a unique ambience. Its precision acoustics give the impression that one could hear a pin drop – even in a crowd of people.

Used primarily to record classical music and prestige artists, it was initially assigned to His Master's Voice – the most prestigious EMI label in the 1930s. One of the few studios in the world that can accommodate an entire orchestra, it is used to record film scores, live concerts, and classical works. Up in the rafters, a projection room survives from its erstwhile conversion into a film-score studio, although films are now projected onto Studio 1's huge rear-wall screen as well as smaller plasma screens throughout the Studio.

For me, Studio 1 is fantastic. You've got the extra reverb if you want it, but you can partition the person you're recording into a hut and screen them off if you want to, too.

John Leckie, producer

Above, left to right:
Hungarian conductor and composer Antal Doráti in Studio 1 with the BBC Symphony Orchestra in the 1960s; A panoramic shot of a grand piano in Studio 1, with its modern-day acoustic panelling
Opposite: *Composer Igor Stravinsky conducts **Les Noces** on 10th July 1934 with the BBC Chorus in Studio 1, with its original art deco features. Joe Batten stands on the left looking up at the rostrum*

As sound recording became a more exacting science, Studio 1 required updating. In 1971, whilst manager of Recording Operations, Ken Townsend was responsible for its renovation. Acoustic panelling was fixed along its walls, with a further series of panels that could be placed in different positions to manipulate the space in the room.

Ken's pavilions

"I redesigned the studio with Peter Dix, who was the acoustics man at Hayes and was brilliant," says Townsend. "It had a reverberation time of 2.4, which was too low for classical recording so we designed all those blue panels that are still there." The pair bought the raw materials needed for the panels in their lunch hour from a hardware company in Islington, then transported them to Hayes for assembly, ready for mounting in Studio 1. "We raised the studio's reverberation time to 3.2 and it proved a great success."

"We also designed a ten by ten feet movable enclosure so we had a small studio within the very big one. This gave us the dual benefit of either a small pop studio or a separation booth for large orchestral sessions. Due to my interest in cricket it became known as Ken's Pavilion."

By the 1980s, fewer bands needed the space or could afford the expense of the largest recording studio in the world – which reduced the number of bookings and led to some unusual goings-on in the vast Studio 1 space.

"It was being used for things like car maintenance, and we used to play badminton in there quite a bit," says Chris Buchanan, former director of operations at the Studios. "That was great fun – I put brass screws down that would line up with where we'd put the masking tape to have a game. Then Ken got to hear about Anvil, and they started recording at Abbey Road and eventually they took the whole thing over. That was really the saving grace for Abbey Road, certainly Studio 1."

Buchanan retired in 2002, when the influence of film was still strong. "We rebuilt the control desk for film that year," he adds, "which has paid dividends."

Above: *Peter Cobbin, Director of Engineering, at the mixing desk in Studio 1.*
Opposite: *The view from the control room in Studio 1, where producers and engineers often sit alongside film directors. The digital screen shows split-second timing enabling them to blend the music with events in the film.*

Studio 2:
the home of pop

Undeniably world-famous, Studio 2 is the original home of pop at Abbey Road. Its design has changed little over the years, and retains the familiar high ceiling and pale walls. Long, brown quilts, filled with wadding and fastened against the walls to dampen the studio's acoustics produce the perfect sound qualities; tall baffles deflect or absorb sound and can also be fixed to the walls to create a single, large space; smaller baffles shield amplifiers and instruments.

Taking control

The striking control room in Studio 2 has bright red walls to inspire and focus engineers and producers at work, along with deep leather sofas to cocoon artists as they listen back at the end of a recording. Accessible from the main hallway, and with a door onto stairs that lead down to the studio's vintage parquet floor, the control room is not an original feature and was installed as part of another Ken Townsend renovation.

"It was originally downstairs and later on we turned it into a pop-designated cutting room," says Townsend. "We put Michael Grafton-Green in there, who was the most unlikely pop disc cutter you could imagine, as his dress was very formal – he always wore a dark blue suit and tie."

"It's become iconic, a monument... a lot more people are aware of it, other than just musicians and studio professionals. It's got a real mystique about it.

John Leckie, producer

A large space such as Studio 2 allows room for plenty of microphones and other equipment to be set up around a band – much of it vintage apparatus from the 1950s, 1960s, and 1970s. The thrill of using instruments and other items featured on iconic recordings from the past adds a special timbre to recordings by modern bands.

"During the 1960s, The Beatles were pushing the boundaries," says technical engineer Lester Smith. "John Lennon always knew what he wanted. He would say, 'Can you make this bit of gear do something different?' and by the next day it would do what he wanted. Then he'd say 'That's great, man'."

Above, clockwise from top left: *Studio 2 laid bare – except for a grand piano; The screens, consoles, and bright red walls of the Studio 2 control room; Microphones ready for action in Studio 2*
Opposite: *Lights, monitors, and microphones are set up by technicians in Studio 2*

It doesn't matter where you stand or where you put the mic in Studio 2, when you put the fader up it always makes you say 'Wow', without a doubt. The room itself is designed to be an amplifier.

John Leckie, producer

The Beatles effect continues

The Beatles set the precedent for experimentation during their tenure in Studio 2 in the 1960s – a tradition that continues to this day. "For a pop session, there's definitely a sense of 'Let's get in a room together, set up, and make an album – let's see what happens'," confirms Mirek Stiles, Head of Audio Products at Abbey Road.

A few individuals who broke the mould some 50 years ago are still playing the game. "I remember one Paul McCartney session where he set up a drum kit in the space between the fire exit and the back door of Studio 2," recalls Stiles. "It's basically a small square room – I'd never seen anyone do that before. It sounded amazing."

A slight problem occurred, however, as the space was not soundproofed. "Then the phone started ringing and it was security, saying the neighbours were complaining about the noise," adds Stiles. "I tried explaining to them that I couldn't go and tell Paul McCartney to stop playing."

At the heart of each Abbey Road studio lies its recording and mixing desk. In Studio 2, the first multi-track desk was delivered from EMI's Record Engineering Development Department in 1958 – the REDD.17 'Stereosonic' console, which used valve technology. Of three machines built, two were installed at Abbey Road and the third was used for location recording. While early Beatles material was recorded and mixed on this desk, the REDD.51 console is most closely linked with the group, arriving in January 1964 – shortly after another unit had been installed in Studio 3. The majority of The Beatles' songs were recorded and mixed on this model, excepting some classical overdubs from Studio 1. The REDD consoles were designed by Peter K. Burkowitz of EMI Electrola in Germany; he produced his first successful model – the REDD.17 – in 1956.

Desk jobs: REDD is replaced by TG

In the late 1960s, EMI's engineers at Hayes were briefed to supply a new series of transistor-designed desks for Abbey Road. The first incarnation, the TG Mk I, was installed in Studio 2 in 1968, with other units placed in Studios 1 and 3 in 1970. The TG console offered greater finesse with its controls, and allowed easier multi-track recording via its eight tracks, either in stereo or on two mono channels.

The Beatles recorded only one album on the TG, but it proved the most integral to the long-term public image of the Studios. In tribute to their recording home, the band named their 1969 release *Abbey Road*. In response, the Studios officially changed its name from 'EMI Studios' to Abbey Road Studios. The album cover showed the now iconic view of the Beatles traversing the zebra crossing on the road in front of the Studios – since honoured time and time again in pastiche.

Above: *(top left) The REDD.51 desk, photographed in 1968, was used by The Beatles to record the bulk of their material, including* **Sgt. Pepper** *(bottom left) The TG Mk I desk, designed by engineers at EMI, which replaced the REDD.51*
Insets, right and opposite: *The Beatles at work with music publisher Dick James and producer George Martin in 1964, behind the REDD.51 mixing desk in Studio 2*

INSIDE THE STUDIOS

237

Studio 3: prog and more

Just as Studio 2 was home to the pop explosion of the 1960s, Studio 3 was the epicentre for 1970s prog rock recorded at Abbey Road. As a young tape operator, one of John Leckie's early assignments in the studio was to assist the recording of George Harrison's ***All Things Must Pass*** solo triple album of 1970, in which the former Beatle had contributions from well-known friends including Ringo Starr, Bob Dylan, and Eric Clapton – with Phil Spector as co-producer.

"Most of what I remember about that session was running around trying to find 25 pairs of headphones that worked," says Leckie. "If one pair wasn't working, they couldn't record and I'd be the one to blame!"

Less is more in the modern age

Transformed from its look in 1931, Studio 3 had a full overhaul under Ken Townsend. In 1988, its mixing desk moved to the opposite end of the room with a relaxation area on the floor above, overlooking the studio. With space for 20 musicians, the room today is tall and bright, with wooden flooring and acoustic panels on the walls. The mirrored back room is popular for recording drums – because drummers are a vain breed, goes the joke among staff.

"By the 1980s, a lot of bands weren't playing at the same time when they were recording, so they didn't need a space that big," says Simon Campbell, Head of Technical Services at Abbey Road. "The control-room space is now as big as the studio itself." With a kitchen and bathroom included, bands can record in private without distractions.

Prog-rock titans and 1970s Abbey Road clients Pink Floyd returned in 1988 as the first band to work in the new-look studio. They mixed their live double release, ***The Delicate Sound of Thunder*** – the first rock album played in space.

Left: *A drum kit lit up in the dazzling mirrored room at the rear of Studio 3*
Opposite: *(main) An engineer adjusts Studio 3's acoustic panels; (far right) Studio 3 in the 1940s, before its renovation in 1988; (below) Setting up and recording in Studio 3*

The Penthouse Studio

odelled from three small post-production rooms, the Penthouse Studio on the second floor added an intimate space to Abbey Road's line-up – an alternative to the small set-ups, which were thriving in competition with the Studios. "I first drew the plans for the Penthouse Studio on the back of a cigarette packet while I was going home on the train," says Ken Townsend. "It's on a floating floor."

First to use the Penthouse Studio in 1981 were British new-wave band A Flock of Seagulls. "Colin Miles who worked at Parlophone wanted to try them out in there," says Townsend, "and when I heard the name I told him they could use it for free provided they didn't leave a deposit on the desk!" Graced also by the likes of The Buzzcocks and The Cure, the Penthouse is now used largely for mastering 5.1 and surround sound in the isolation booth, and mixing film scores on the only digital mixing desk at the complex. A 48-track Neve Capricorn console was introduced in 1992; the current model is the DFC Gemini.

On the opposite side of the Penthouse Studio lie three cutting rooms, where Townsend raised productivity by requiring engineers to work a 70-hour week, followed by a week off. The studio was refitted in 1996, with further updating in 2007. Mixing, mastering, and remastering also take place in a further 17 rooms in the complex, along with recently added facilities for video and the Abbey Road Online Mixing and Online Mastering websites.

Opposite, main and insets:
The Penthouse control room, where celebrities recorded war poetry for **We Will Remember Them** *in 2010, in aid of Help for Heroes and The Royal British Legion*
Above, from left:
The Penthouse mixing desk; The control room viewed from behind a speaker

Inside the
echo chamber

Tucked behind Studio 2 lies Echo Chamber 2 – the only one still in use at Abbey Road. Soundproofed, dimly lit, and clammy, it feels remote from the buzz of the rest of the Studios – the air tinged with the odour of seeping damp. The gloomy booth of today in fact pioneered modern recording technology – as with many architectural relics at Abbey Road. Dating back to the site's original remodelling in 1931, the electro-acoustic echo chambers of Abbey Road were among the first in the world to be purpose-built for sound recording – with a chamber for each studio space. Such structures were the special-effects devices of their day, adding depth to a recording, or suggesting the acoustics of a large concert hall.

Opposite: *Echo Chamber 2 – the pipes pictured were replaced by white ones with a grey trim as part of the Beatles remastering project in the mid-1990s*
Left: *The echo chamber today*
Inset: *The 'echo patching room' in 1968 – used to capture recordings from within Echo Chamber 2*

Bouncing sound around

Unlike a recording studio, an echo chamber has reflective surfaces to cause soundwaves to bounce and reverberate, routed in via a loudspeaker and recaptured by a microphone. Echo Chamber 2 has tiled and painted walls, while floor-to-ceiling sewer pipes increase reverberations. Up on the rooftop of the building is another echo chamber. Presently used for storage it also houses four EMT 140 Echo Plates, and remains fit for use when it's needed.

> Eventually they were able to dig out and refurbish the second chamber to make it work for us the way it used to, even to the extent of putting back a lot of the old metalwork sewage pipes, which were originally glazed and actually contributed to the chamber's acoustic qualities.

Sir George Martin, on remastering material for *The Beatles Anthology*

The Mobile Unit: Studios on tour

O ne recording studio not always housed at Abbey Road is its Mobile Recording Unit. The spirit of Fred Gaisberg and his early sound engineers lives on through its operations.

Richard Hale, who joined Abbey Road in 1968, was instrumental in reviving the Mobile Unit's fortunes in the early 1970s. "My colleague Graham Kirkby and I asked Ken Townsend if we could do location recording full-time. By 1974 we had our first Mercedes van, which has been one of many," he says. The Unit was further transformed when they were given flight cases to carry their material – a working practice that has continued. "It was predominantly live shows and classical recordings, so it became much more convenient to take into a chapel, theatre, club, or concert hall," says Hale. "And it's still like that today."

One curious tale survives of a van housing the Mobile Unit of 1931. "We had a van that caught fire in the garage," says Townsend. "We don't know what caused it – it's a bit of an odd one. It suddenly burnt up one night and took the roof of the garage off." One suspect factor was the wax stored on board, ready for recording.

Left: *The black Lancia vans of the first EMI Mobile Unit of 1931. Later units had 'By Royal Appointment' crests on the front and rear, after being used to record waxes of the monarch's speeches.*
Right: *An engineer works in the Mobile Recording Unit in 1948*
Far right: *(top) A REDD.37 desk, 4-track Studer, and BTR tape machines from 1968 – all of which went on the road with the Mobile Unit; (below) Italian conductor Riccardo Muti, Tony Caronia – Director of Angel Records, East Coast North America, assistant engineer Mark Vigars, location technical engineer Richard Hale, and EMI producer John Willan in Philadelphia with a TG Mk 2 desk – which was modified for location recording*

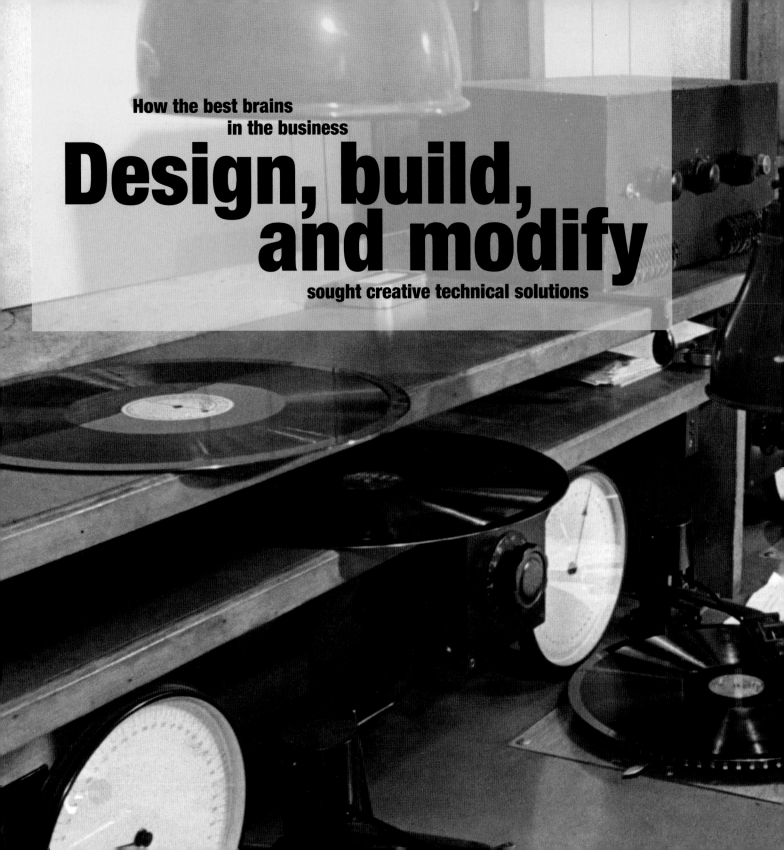

How the best brains
in the business

Design, build,
and modify

sought creative technical solutions

The history of magnetic tape

One of the most durable formats for recording music, magnetic tape was developed in its modern form by German engineers during the 1930s. Following the Second World War, a team of audio engineers from the United States and the United Kingdom – which included E.W. Berth-Jones from Abbey Road – travelled to Germany in 1946 to study the tape's recording system.

EMI's engineers set to work at their Research Laboratories in Hayes, Middlesex, creating the first British Tape Recorder machine – the BTR1 – in 1947, primarily for use in-house and at the BBC. Introduced at Abbey Road in October 1948, the new technology was initially used as a back-up to wax discs. The machines recorded onto premium professional magnetic EMITAPE – the primary medium used for recordings at Abbey Road by the 1950s.

By 1972, EMI were advertising their latest tape in *Gramophone* magazine: "a professional audio recording tape offering extremely low noise and low print-through performance coupled with the advantages of a matt-coated back. After years of research, the company has been able drastically to reduce the four main inherent noise factors affecting magnetic tape – bias, bulk erase, amplitude modulation, and frequency modulation effects."

Above and opposite:
Abbey Road engineers work in control rooms installed with BTR1 tape machines. The BTR series were known as 'green machines' because of their distinctive paintwork.

Terrific tape

With the advent of magnetic tape, engineers could register multiple takes without greatly increasing the cost of the recording, while performances could be enhanced by cutting and rejoining the tape to edit out any mistakes. For broadcasting purposes, material could be pre-recorded at the Studios, releasing radio artists from the strains of live performance and gaining more control over the quality and pace of their material. Artists could also record for longer periods than on wax discs. A particular satisfaction was the clarity of recording on magnetic tape – still sought after for its warm tone and high fidelity to this day. It also remains one of the most durable materials on which to record.

Problems we might have with old analogue tape include it and its edits falling apart, but we also have tape from the 1950s that plays beautifully and sounds great.

Sean Magee, Abbey Road sound engineer

Splicing magnetic tape

Unlike wax discs, magnetic tape can be edited because it is possible to physically alter its playing surface without denigrating the fidelity of the recording it bears. Physical edits on tape are known as splices and are typically created on an editing block, which holds the tape in place while it is cut. The two loose ends of the tape are then butted together and joined with splicing tape – a special adhesive tape that does not impede the magnetic tape's functionality.

Splices on magnetic tape are typically cut with a sharp blade and at an angle, which dissipates the noise created by the slice across the recording, rendering it less noticeable. Editing scissors were commonly used as they allowed the adjustment of the angle of the cut across the tape. Splices can also be used to create intentional effects on recordings – a diagonal splice on a stereo recording will begin on one channel a split second before the other, while a particularly long, angled splice will create a dissolve effect from one sound to the next. Magnetic tape can also accommodate multiple parallel tracks, and thus was the first recording medium to allow stereo and multi-track recordings – offering artists and producers greater avenues for experimentation.

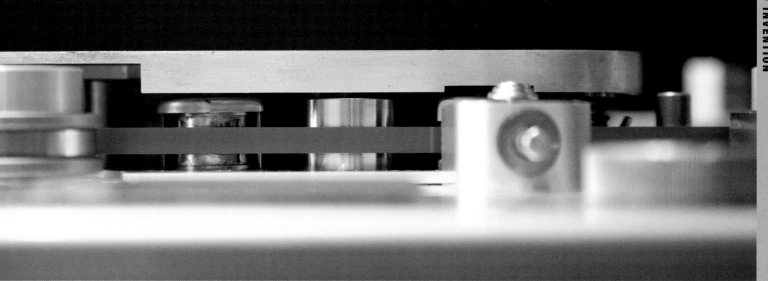

Studer steps up tape machine technology

The manufacturing market outside EMI adjusted as recording on magnetic tape became more commonplace. Eventually, the Studios bought in tape machines designed by Swiss company Studer. These were initially used alongside the BTR machines designed by EMI, but eventually replaced them.

Studer pioneered multi-track tape machines with its J37 model in 1964. Abbey Road installed them soon afterwards, and the J37 is famous for being used on The Beatles' 1967 album *Sgt. Pepper*. The J37 was a four-track recorder, but later machines accommodated eight, sixteen, and twenty-four tracks (the latter eventually becoming standard for analogue recordings). For adventurous artists, multi-track recording consoles could be engineered to send multiple tracks to the Studer tape machine as a single input – sacrificing some fidelity, but enabling analogue recording where the number of tracks on the desk was multiplied by the tape machine's number of inputs.

The distinctive Studer design consists of a familiar reel-to-reel set-up for the tape, featuring a built-in cutting mechanism so that the tape can remain in place to complete the edit. The front of the machine displays a series of inputs, which are numbered sequentially in large white letters on a black background. As with other equipment used in sound recording, later models used transistors rather than the early valve system. Later innovations also included electronically controlled tape tension, tape timing, and speed control. Preset levels and other features were easily accessible on plug-in units next to the meters.

If you play an old tape on a new tape machine, there's a danger you'll get the wrong information. It's like they speak different languages.

Simon Gibson,
Abbey Road audio restoration and mastering engineer

Direct-to-disc
recording

efore the widespread use of magnetic tape at Abbey Road from the 1950s, engineers recorded 'direct to disc'. This required the sound from the performance in the studio to be channelled through a cutting lathe directly onto a wax disc. Without the luxury of playback before the creation of the master recording, commercial releases using this method put the onus on artists achieving a recording in a single take – with no post-production tinkering in edits, multi-track, or overdubs. Even stereophonic sound was mixed in real time.

A purist's dream... but a performer's nightmare

For some there is charm in the spontaneous live-performance fidelity of a direct-to-disc recording – more so than in engineered analogue or digital recordings. Even so, the terror of a disc-cutting glitch over a long recording ensures modern long-playing records' impracticality for artists and engineers alike. Despite valve-powered equipment having been rendered obsolescent, and solid-state cutting lathes now accommodating vinyl, magnetic tape and the LP format finally sounded the death knell of direct-to-disc for all but the most hardy audiophile.

Above: *Abbey Road engineer Edward 'Chick' Fowler operates a cutting lathe in the 1930s*

Opposite: *Two engineers replace the valve on the amplifier on an early cutting lathe. Valves were replaced with transistors in later 'solid-state' models.*

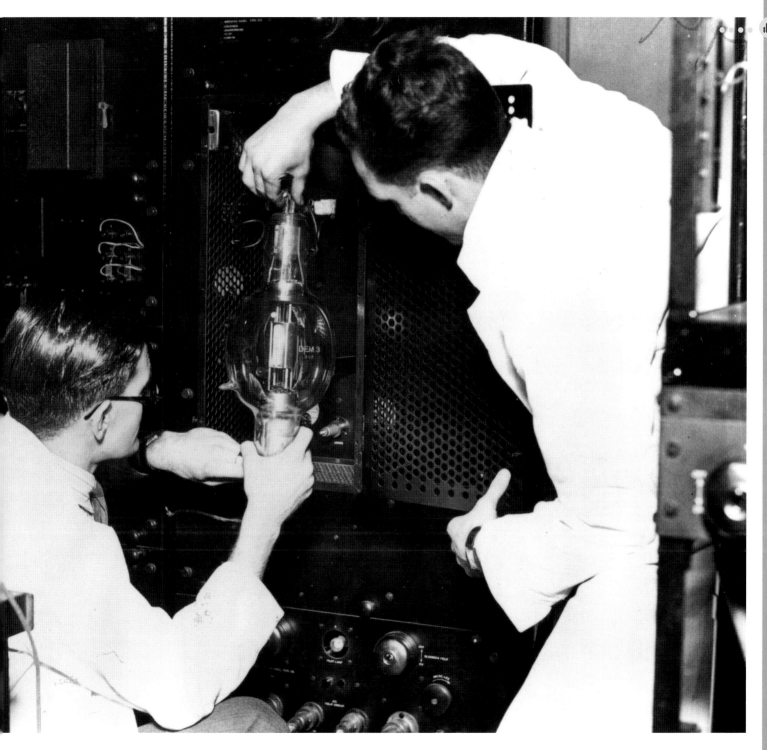

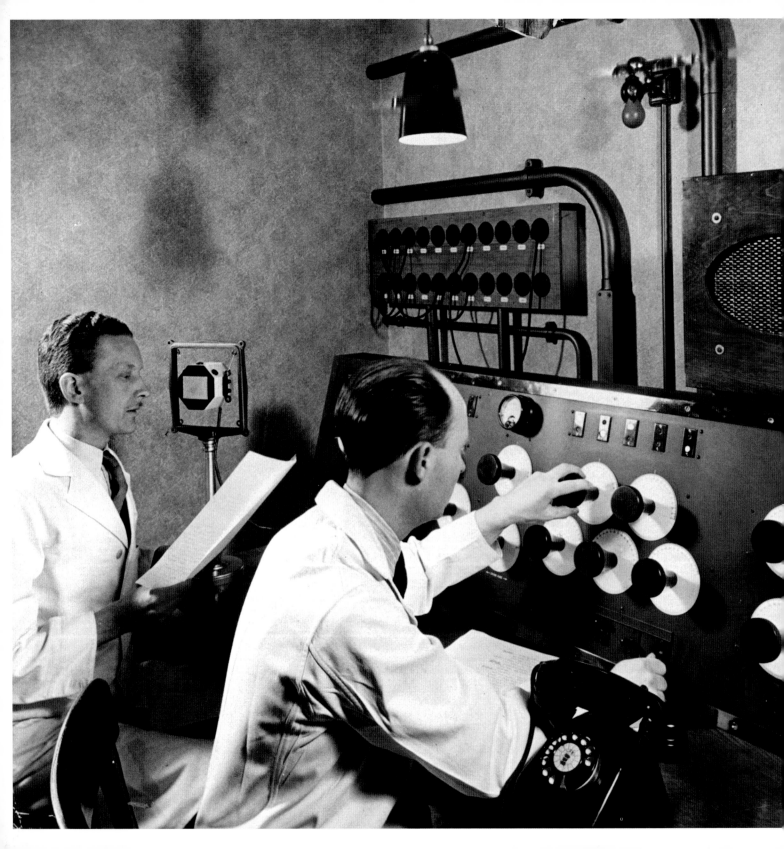

Audio recordings in the mix

arly recording techniques at Abbey Road Studios laid the blueprints for analogue mixing consoles, or mixing desks, which slowly evolved into current-day digital versions. Prior to the 1930s, acoustic recording onto wax discs simply reproduced sound as it was captured – with no frills. Via the console or desk in the control room, however, the arrival of electrical recording onto tape allowed engineers to mix and adjust different input signals – and in later versions introduce audio effects to a recording.

Early mixing consoles predated magnetic tape, stereo, and multi-track recording. They were primarily designed to capture the performance of sizeable groups such as orchestras in a large space that amplified the sound. The subsequent emergence of pop music and spoken-word recordings arguably hastened the evolution of the mixing console, as they called for 'close-up' recording and more adventurous manipulation of fewer instruments.

At Abbey Road, the specialist staff operating its consoles were able to develop techniques particular to the venue's acoustics in its bespoke studios, in combination with the very latest in sound technology. Abbey Road's studio recordings share a trademark subtlety of tone and sound, quite distinct from the recordings captured in concert halls or churches. Alongside the vocal, instrumental, and other elements in a recording, sound engineers – via the mixing desk – play no small part in crafting the final edit that goes to print: capturing, balancing, and refining the specific aural effects of each room. The need for close collaboration between highly skilled engineers and talented artists requires great respect on both sides in order to achieve the optimal end product.

Opposite: *Recording engineer Edward 'Chick' Fowler (left) and balance engineer Laurie Bamber work at a mixing console in the 1930s. Receiving an input signal from the microphone on the desk, the red bulb overhead indicated when a recording was in progress.*

By EMI, for Abbey Road Studios: the TG desks

With console technology still in its relative infancy, EMI specialists at their base in Hayes, Middlesex, created an improved mixing desk for use at Abbey Road. Designed to a 1967 brief from Studios' engineers, the TG12345 mixing desk accommodated a larger number of inputs than preceding models to better facilitate multi-track recording. This new recording desk could also record simultaneously in stereo.

The TG featured stud switches on most of its rotary controls and quadrant faders – a progression from the dials on early mixing consoles, which offered accurate calibration during the mixing process. Other innovations included the use of transformers on all inputs and outputs, and a compressor/limiter on audio channels.

The versatility of the TG desks led to their popularity with pop bands famed for their experimentation, such as The Beatles (on *Abbey Road*) and Pink Floyd (on *Dark Side of the Moon*). Also suited to orchestral recordings, the desks were used in Studio 1 for both classical sessions and film score work.

Before being decommissioned in 1983, the TG went through four versions. The only version not installed at Abbey Road was the Mk III, which was manufactured for use in EMI's international studios. Only two Mk IV desks were produced – both for Abbey Road. The superseded Mk I and Mk II desks were modified for use mainly in mobile units – a requirement in the engineers' original design brief. The quality build and flexibility of the TG desk ensured its longevity and it remains in demand today.

Opposite and right, top to bottom: *A selection of faders, switches, and dials on a TG desk at Abbey Road. The desk features a microphone that the engineer or producer can activate to speak to the artist in the studio from the control room.*

Mastering: the console

Above: *(left) A close-up shot of the monitor on a TG12410 transfer console; (right) 'Chicken feet' buttons on the console*

Opposite: *The TG12410 transfer console, which has been used daily since its installation in the early 1970s, and is rarely switched off*

The long-standing Abbey Road Studios tradition of using custom-built technology survives to this day. The EMI TG mixing desks may have been supplanted by models from British companies Neve and SSL, but some vintage TG equipment remains in constant use – such as the TG12410 transfer console. Designed by former Abbey Road chief engineer Mike Batchelor and his colleagues, the desk was installed in six of the mastering suites in the 70s to optimize transfer of audio signals to vinyl.

Like all TG models, it is a solid-state design rather than a valve desk and features the familiar components of equalizers, compressor/limiters, input units, filters, and vertical amplitude limiters – as well as monitoring and check units. Alongside it sits a 'Moscow Box' router – another item of equipment dreamed up at the Studios, which enables the mastering engineer to monitor any digital source and to select the digital processing required.

With modern-day technology, recordings can be mastered in both mono and stereo and, significantly, can be sanctioned by a second pair of specialist ears prior to release. Remastering a recording – where possible using the same equipment as the original – requires a delicate balance between updating a classic recording while preserving its well-loved character.

A recent Abbey Road refinement is an online mastering and mixing service, offering expert input to bands or artists who lack the time or finances to travel to the Studios.

A legend of bricks and baffles

On first entering Studio 2, musicians are often awed by the vestiges of all the iconic artists who have previously recorded there. Equipped with endless possibilities for tuning the acoustics, the studio has walls with bricks laid end on – an unusual design that ingeniously muffles the transition of sound and vibration to neighbouring studios; the doors to the room are also densely insulated. The heavy, ribbed floor-to-ceiling brown panels around the sides of the room are quilts filled with wadding and fastened flush against the walls to dampen the studio's acoustics.

Acoustic baffles – tall, white perforated screens – are fixed along two walls, mounted on castors to swing into different arrangements to alter the studio's dimensions; smaller versions are often erected on rugs closer to the centre of the studio. Baffles minimize noise pollution, and can be angled to alter the refraction of sound. For a more intimate sound environment, technicians use baffle boards to create artificial isolation booths.

To add an extra Studio 2 frisson, artists can also book instruments from its collection. These include a Steinway Model D concert grand piano and the legendary 'Mrs Mills' upright Steinway piano. The latter was named for Gladys Mills, who recorded some 40 albums of honky-tonk piano music for EMI on the instrument in the 1960s and early 1970s.

Opposite, clockwise from left: *Unique 'endways' brickwork creates dense internal walls; The Studio 2 control room, walls fitted with red cloth panels; The tall, white, wall-mounted baffles and brown acoustic panels in Studio 2; A vertical view of a tall baffle; Studio 2's stairway leads down from its control room to the studio floor; Bolts secure the baffles' panelling; A close-up view of the keyboard of the 'Mrs Mills' piano, famously favoured by the Beatles for its hard sound and pleasantly 'off-key' tuning; A close-up shot of the quilted acoustic panels; The lighting board in Studio 2*

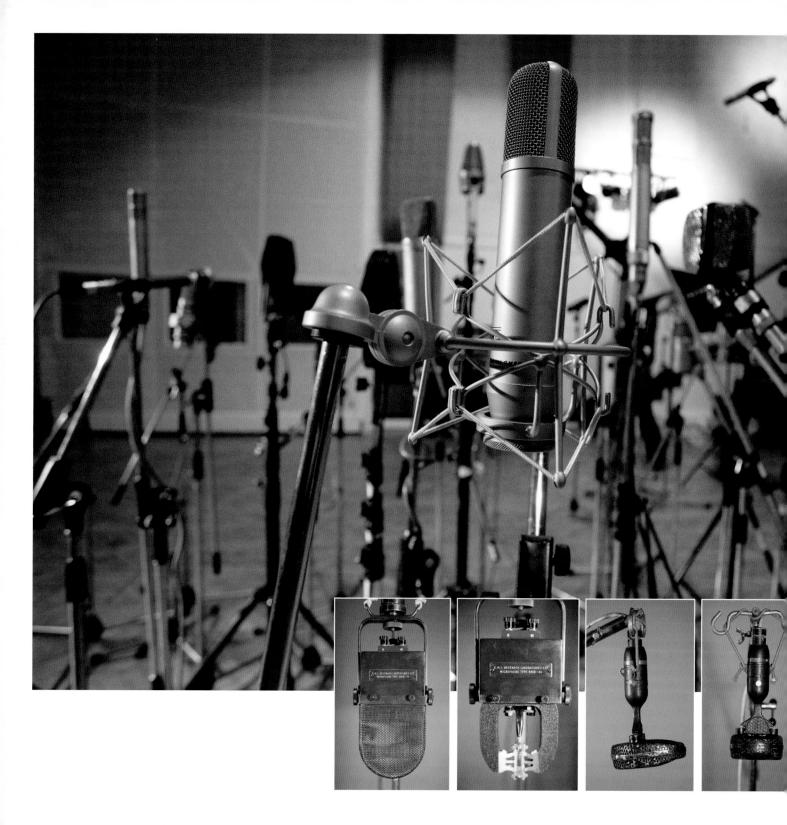

Microphones
virtual and vintage

ans all over the world can now use Abbey Road facilities, via plug-ins in digital packages such as **ProTools** – including multiple microphone styles. Artists who come to the Studios in person, however, can enjoy the real thing – from every era. "We've not got rid of any vintage microphones," says Lester Smith, an Abbey Road engineer specializing in microphone restoration. "They go back 60 years and they're in use every day."

Getting technical

In the early days, microphones were built in-house by EMI, but from the end of the Second World War, the Studios looked elsewhere. "We bought the best equipment available," says Smith. "After the War, you couldn't typically go out and buy anything, but with microphones there were quite a few companies who manufactured them, particularly Neumann in Germany and AKG in Austria. After the war we bought the first microphones Neumann produced: the U47, U48, M49, and M50." Initially model numbers referred to the year of design but by producing several models in the same year, this rule soon broke down.

In 1972 the Technical Services Department was created and Smith was called from the cutting room to join as in-house microphone specialist. "Before then, technical people who worked in the Studios were in charge of fixing everything," he says, and his early training in several areas at Abbey Road makes him unique within the current technical team.

Above: *(left) A mid-1930s British-made STC 4021 dynamic moving-coil microphone (nick-named the ball and biscuit); (right) A rare AKG D30 from the late 50s*
Opposite, main: *A selection of vintage and modern microphones, ready for use in Studio 2*
Insets, left to right:
A 1948 EMI RM1B ribbon microphone, covered and exposed; Front and side views of a BBC-designed STC 4038 studio ribbon microphone from 1953; AKG's C24 stereo microphone from the 1970s

> They offered me the choice between microphones or tape machines, and I plumped for microphones because I was already experienced with tape machines and wanted something different.

Lester Smith, Abbey Road technical engineer

The classic sound of vintage

Microphone technology at Abbey Road Studios is remarkable in that it has both moved on – and stood still. Today, vintage and new microphones are used in tandem. "In every session we do, at least 25 to 30% of the microphones are vintage models," says Lester Smith. "Vintage microphones tend to be used on the front-line instruments, soloists and singers where they can enrich certain qualities from each, and later microphones will be used on everything else."

Access to rare, well-built equipment is unusual, but vintage microphones are often sought because of the unique way each model conveys its frequency response. "The new microphones aren't inferior," explains Smith. "The aim with recording is to get as true a sound as possible. Microphones all sound a little bit different to each other, though, and the microphone is the most difficult to design to reproduce sound faithfully". Smith cites Brüel & Kjær microphones – originally manufactured for scientific use – as recording a relatively flat frequency which is nearly identical to the original sound.

Fashions change over what is regarded as pleasing: 1990s recordings revived the 1960s tendency to record through microphones with a bright top end. "During the 1990s in particular," recalls Smith, "young bands wanted to sound like the artists who recorded here in the 1960s."

Above all, Abbey Road is a universal studio catering for all tastes. Some engineers like a particular sound and will ask for the B&K microphones, while others prefer a more mellow-sounding microphone.

Clockwise, from bottom left: *Opera singer Jussi Björling records into the 1934 HB1E moving-coil microphone designed by Alan Blumlein at EMI; Glenn Miller and Dinah Shore pose in front of a HB1E; Actress Dame Margaret Rutherford records into a binaural set-up of two microphones – here a 1940s STC 4033 composite microphone and a 1960s Neumann U67 multi-directional condenser microphone – providing an early form of stereo; A young Cliff Richard sings into a similar binaural set-up; The Beverley Sisters record binaurally; Abbey Road engineers erect microphones in Studio 1; Actors Lynn and Michael Redgrave record into another Neumann microphone*

Above: *(left) Cradles for Neumann microphones in Lester Smith's Abbey Road office; (right) 1968 Neumann condenser KM 86 microphones in their drawer*
Below: *(from left) STC 4033 combined dynamic and ribbon microphone, 1940s; Unusual Neumann condenser microphone U47p with Torpedo Head M5 1955/6; Neumann condenser microphone U67, 1960*
Opposite: *Howard Jones (left) and Joe Loss at the mic; (inset) A 1931 EMI HB1E dynamic microphone*

Three main types of microphone are in common use at Abbey Road Studios. Ribbon microphones arrived in the late 1920s and have a warm sound. They are typically very fragile and must be handled with care. "The ribbon is a little strip of corrugated foil," explains Lester Smith. "It's why they say never blow into a microphone, because you can destroy the ribbon that way." The ribbon microphone was later further refined by EMI engineer Alan Blumlein to enable binaural sound – an early form of stereo – utilizing two ribbons known as a Blumlein pair.

Dynamic microphones are based on the principle of sound falling upon a diaphragm which induces a signal into a coil of wire by means of electromagnetic induction. In 1931 Alan Blumlein considerably improved on the design and because of their durability and high gain before feedback, dynamic microphones are to this day the most popular type of microphone for live use.

Condenser microphones, invented in 1916, produce a high-quality audio signal covering the entire sonic spectrum. Vibrations cause the space between internal plates to vary, in a process known as capacitance change. Condenser microphones use either valve or transistor technology. Valve models are heavy, fragile and subtly colour the sound so that each microphone has its own unique character. Modern transistor models are small, light and offer purity and accuracy. "After years of everything being transistorized some people were saying 'We do like the old valve sound', says Smith, "so companies like Neumann and AKG have produced new microphones that have gone back to valve technology." Modern transistor microphones are smaller, lighter, and need less maintenance – but the charisma of vintage microphones lives on. "Now I've got examples of our most famous microphones that are valve microphones, and modern-day Neumann equivalents," says Smith. "Microphones are unique in the world of electronic items, as there are still models that are very popular after 60 years."

The unsung heroes

Behind the scenes

of Abbey Road Studios' success

The people who make Abbey Road

From the tea ladies to the technicians, each and every Abbey Road member of staff has played a part in creating the multitude of hits recorded at the Studios.

On the ground floor, and opening to the garden, lies its stylish private restaurant. Rebuilt by Ken Townsend as a simple canteen when he took over as General Manager, it provides space for staff and clients to eat, drink, and relax during breaks or at the end of the day. "I tried to change the way we treated people," says Townsend. "We started giving artists flowers and put bowls of fruit out in the studios. The restaurant meant you could have a bite to eat, rather than have to go round the corner to a café. The technical staff could never get out, so before that they could never eat at work."

Health, safety, shotguns, and the bar

The new facilities were not without their teething problems – in particular an ill-timed visit from Health and Safety officials. "The day they came, the drains were blocked, so there was waste running down the corridors," recalls Townsend.

The restaurant also includes a licensed bar. "Linda McCartney once said to me, 'That'll be the worst thing you ever do, Ken!' and there were times I thought she was right," he adds, declining to name and shame any miscreants.

Such issues pale compared with the problems Abbey Road has had with some of its neighbours. One arrived late at night to complain about the noise – armed with a shotgun!

Above: *Dolly Wheeler serves a cup of tea to André Previn in the Abbey Road canteen during the early 1970s – she asked whether he was a musician*
Right: *The first female cutting engineer at Abbey Road – celebrated for her sense of humour – Hazel Yarwood operates a lathe on a 1960s release*

> Before we had the restaurant, you could only get a drink late at night if security let you into the kitchen. They'd stand by you while you made tea in cups and saucers for everyone in the session at five o'clock in the morning.

John Leckie, producer

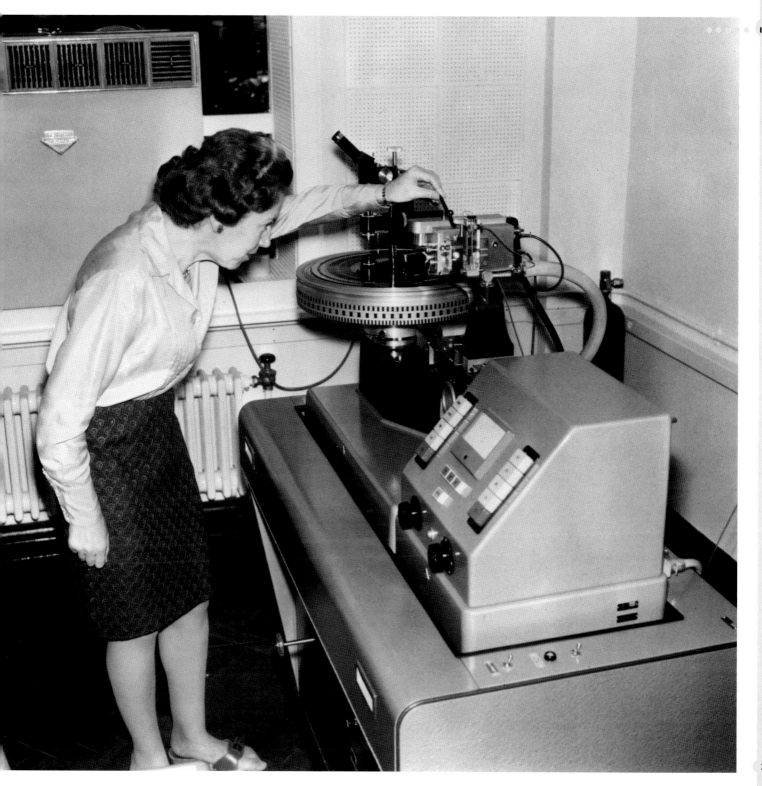

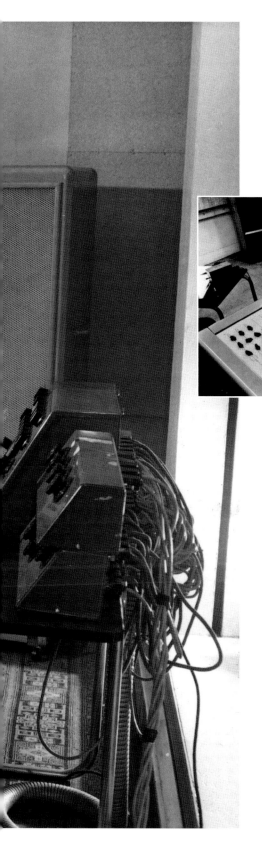

Giants of pop engineering

As Abbey Road became the studio of choice for musicians, so too its top engineers came to enjoy a considerable influence – as they transformed the world of recorded music.

One of the earliest specialist pop engineers, Malcolm Addey, pioneered 'close mixing' – resulting in louder, more intimate recordings. Norman Newell was already a well-connected figure in the music industry before his appointment in 1949 as an A&R manager for Columbia. Abbey Road encouraged him to develop the genre of cast recordings of popular musicals from Britain and America. His distinguished career as a producer and songwriter continued until his retirement in 1990.

Another important contributor at Abbey Road was Gus Cook, who began his career at the Studios on the day it opened. He eventually graduated to become its General Manager in 1969, before retirement in 1974. Cook was present for many recording milestones such as the invention of stereo by Alan Blumlein, the introduction of magnetic tape, and the adoption of lacquer masters. A progressive, he abolished the Studios' strict dress code during his time in charge and instituted a programme to transfer old 78rpm recordings onto tape for possible re-release – anticipating Abbey Road's later remastering initiative.

Above, from left: *Engineer Ron Pender frequently served as first assistant to the legendary producer Norman 'Hurricane' Smith, shown here at the desk in Studio 2; Gus Cook works at a 24-input, 16-stage mixer in Studio 3, prior to its renovation*
Opposite: *Malcolm Addey, Norman Newell, and engineer Peter Bown work together in the control room of Studio 2, circa 1960*

Engineers as standard-bearers

The 1960s drive to move away from tradition resulted in the rise of several notable engineers. One such was Norman Smith – an RAF pilot during the Second World War who joined Abbey Road in 1959 as an apprentice sound engineer. Smith worked on The Beatles' recordings until 1965, during which time he was given his affectionately ironic nickname 'Hurricane' by John Lennon because of his unhurried, meticulous working habits. From 1965, Smith replaced George Martin as the head of Parlophone and produced various bands – most famously Pink Floyd.

A musician himself, Smith also wrote 'the Beatles song that never was' after the band expressed an interest in a track he had written and offered him £15,000 for it. However, the absence of a song for Ringo Starr on the album in question meant that they instead filled the gap with one of their own compositions. Smith eventually had a brush with the pop charts in 1971 with the No. 2 single *Don't Let It Die*, recorded under the pseudonym Hurricane Smith. This was nearly denied him, as EMI only released the song on the insistence of producer Mickie Most, who correctly predicted that it would would be a Top-Three hit and offered to release it himself if EMI did not.

Two more pop engineers also had an impact – Peter Bown and Stuart Eltham. The former established himself as a skilled engineer on numerous 1970s prog-rock releases – in particular the early albums of Pink Floyd. Eltham was particularly fêted for his experiments with magnetic tape, creating many of the strange effects that became trademarks of comedy records by the likes of Peter Sellers, Spike Milligan, and Peter Ustinov. He also became an accomplished classical music engineer in the 1970s.

Peter Vince was another Abbey Road engineer who facilitated some unorthodox recording techniques, on one occasion helping Australian entertainer Rolf Harris record the vocals for his song *In the Wet* with his face half-submerged in a bowl of water. Vince's apprenticeship at the Studios meant he was multi-skilled – trained in tape operating and disc-cutting, as well as working as a balance engineer. He eventually became another of the Studios' celebrated pop producers.

Insets, above from left: *Peter Bown and cutting engineer Hazel Yarwood behind two BTR machines in the Studio 3 control room in 1951; Stuart Eltham at an early RS 70 8 channel mono mixer in the original Studio 2 control room; Peter Vince works with Cliff Richard, Hank Marvin, and Bruce Welch*

Opposite: *Norman Smith sits alongside 1960s recording artist Johnny Angel*

The boys in the back room

The REDD mixing desks first used at Abbey Road from the late 1950s took their name from the team that created them. An acronym based on EMI's Record Engineering Development Department based in Hayes, Middlesex, the group was set up in 1955 to furnish EMI studios with bespoke apparatus using the latest technology. The REDD.17 console was the first model installed at Abbey Road – one item of equipment out of more than a hundred produced by the team.

From time to time, the Abbey Road engineers themselves came up with revolutionary ideas, driving forward much of the technology used inside the recording studios. Officially forbidden by the management from implementing their own improvements, engineers inevitably bent the rules on occasion.

"We were a bit of a law unto ourselves, but we didn't overstep the mark," says Ken Townsend. "After I invented automatic double-tracking, I got a memo telling us we weren't allowed to do that sort of thing. Then we got another memo saying that they wanted to test it out fully before we could use it again," he adds. "The same night there was a Beatles session and they wanted to use ADT, so of course we used it."

Above: *Two engineers at EMI's Record Engineering Development Department monitor audio quality using sets of early headphones*
Opposite: *Another REDD engineer inspects the groove on a vinyl record cut for the HMV label*

Multi-tracks

Clockwise, from above left: *Two Record Engineering Development Department engineers test out some early model REDD compressors; Two REDD engineers test the response of its early technology; the Neve DFC Gemini desk in the Penthouse Studio*

The early REDD mixing consoles contained amplifiers, but still used valve rather than transistor technology. Built in connecting modules for easy disassembly and transportation, the first model – the REDD.17 – was used for mobile recordings as well as in the Studios. Later models of the REDD desks also had physically interchangeable equalizer modules, optimized for classical and pop recordings. When its eight channels proved insufficient for multi-track recording, the EMI design department developed a sub-mixer to add another four – an indication that multi-track recording was about to grow, in every sense.

Innovation

Abbey Road Studios has a celebrated history of innovation and today's engineers continue to develop breakthroughs in recording and recording technology. In the 1990's Peter Cobbin, now Director of Engineering, introduced 5.1 mixing to the studios and remixed The Beatles original multitracks of Yellow Submarine in 5.1. More recently, the advent of plugin technology in digital recording has reignited interest in vintage Abbey Road Studios equipment. Cobbin has overseen the implementation of successful Abbey Road Studios plugins including the TG12413 limiter, the RS127 and RS124 compressors. "Now everyone's adopting them. Audio plugins gives you fantastic emulations of legendary equipment," says Mirek Stiles, "There's a nostalgic love of that equipment, so people want to be able to record with it."

> "I think what people strive for here is to find new sounds and experiment. As an engineer you have to think, 'Great, let's do this.'
>
> **Mirek Stiles, Abbey Road Head of Audio Products**

Past and present

Part of the reason Abbey Road has so many specialists is because of its low staff turnover. Ken Townsend joined EMI at Hayes in 1950 as a design and development trainee and moved to Abbey Road in 1954 from the Research Division. He joined the Technical Department, known as The Amp Room due to its association with a room that housed amplifiers for the early cutting lathes. His role as recording engineer was primarily to prepare each session technically, including putting out all the microphones, and operating the tape machines on mobile sessions. "I rather liked it up here when I visited – it was sort of a secret place that nobody was ever allowed inside," he says. Townsend is also known as the man who rectified one of The Beatles' few grave concerns about the Studios. "Just after I'd been promoted, I was asked to go to Studio 2 to see them," he says. "John Lennon said, 'Mr Townsend, we have a very serious complaint. The toilet rolls in this place are too hard and shiny. Not only that, but every roll has got 'EMI Ltd' stamped on it.' I walked out of there with my legs shaking, sent someone out to get some softer stuff, and replaced every toilet roll in the place." Townsend held on to that original toilet roll as a souvenir and, in 1980, included it as part of the Studios' Sale of the Century – an auction held to raise money and clear out all the equipment from the recently closed Decca Studios and which included several redundant items from Abbey Road. The toilet roll sold for £80 and, despite appearances on eBay, remains with the son of the original buyer.

Today's Amp Room

Each member of the Technical Services team has their own area of expertise in addition to a broad and deep comprehension of relevant technologies and philosophies both old and new. They carry out key tasks, such as design and installation works, in addition to maintaining all of the Studios equipment.

Clockwise, from far left:

Ken Townsend as 'the world's highest-paid gravedigger' in the 1976 production of **Macula** *at the EMI Elstree Studios; Lucy Launder and Colette Barber; Mastering engineer Chris Blair, who had a 35-year career at the Studios; Celebrated classical producer Walter Legge, who worked at Abbey Road for over 25 years; the technical support team; Oscar Preuss – one of Abbey Road's top producers in the 1940s, and Parlophone's manager before George Martin*

It's a first-class studio all around, from their engineers to the equipment, rooms, and cappuccinos. And of course, feeling the energy of music icons who've recorded there in the past such as the Beatles and Pink Floyd as you walk through the halls doesn't hurt either!

Sunny Park, Executive In Charge of Music at DreamWorks Animation

The team of highly skilled engineers at Abbey Road Studios spans both the studios for recording and mixing, and the mastering suites for mastering and remastering. The studio engineers work across the four studios with composers, artists and producers and are tasked with optimizing and capturing the sound the client creates. Mastering finalizes the recording for production, amending levels, turning it into a smooth listening experience whilst remastering sessions restore older recordings for reissue, with the ability to improve and adapt older recordings for both stereo and surround systems. "We're very different from other facilities because we have our own in-house engineers,"

"In the changing world of music, Abbey Road Studios continues to adapt and evolve whilst retaining a focus on its tradition and reputation for being at the heart of recorded music."

Kerin McDonald, Head of Brand and Marketing

says Colette Barber – the current Studio Manager. "They're absolutely fantastic and very skilled at what they do. Abbey Road accommodates so many different types of recording that you need engineers with specialisms in certain areas."

Nowadays, the range of recordings at Abbey Road Studios includes a vast spectrum of music genres, film scores, computer gaming, classical, jazz, hip-hop, rock and pop and orchestral overdubs. "Also, our engineers know how to get the best out of all these rooms," says Colette. "They know what microphones to use and they know what's hidden away, like the vintage microphones EMI actually built, which we tend to let only our engineers use."

In demand

Colette Barber and Lucy Launder, Post-Production Manager, find an important part of the job is to pair up a client with an appropriate engineer, ensuring their specialist skills match the requirements of the client. Strong working partnerships are formed and frequently, the loyalties of these collaborative bonds are maintained with a series of projects being recorded, mixed, or mastered at the studios. Lucy notes, "We have such a strong team of in-house engineers who are in constant demand."

Studios, post-production and beyond

The pioneering nature carries on with the advent of online mixing, online mastering and remote recording meaning that anyone anywhere in the world can access the expertise of the engineers and Abbey Road Studios equipment. Further initiatives by the senior management team are taking Abbey Road Studios beyond its walls and include the development of Abbey Road Studios licensed products, online and digital applications; including the ever popular webcam, educational initiatives, partnerships that support emerging talent and nurture new music, a successful events business and branded performances and broadcasts, in and out of the Studios.

Abbey Road Studios is one of the only places in the world that represents all that is great about Britain's musical past, present and future. It is a very special and unique place. Everyone who works here feels it and respects that.

Jonathan Smith, SVP EMI Studios

Top row, from left: *Recording and mixing engineers Andrew Dudman, Arne Akselberg, Chris Bolster, Jonathan Allen, Lewis Jones, Sam Okell, Simon Kiln, Simon Rhodes, Peter Cobbin, Gordon Davidson, John Barrett, Paul Pritchard*
Bottom row, from left: *Mastering engineers Adam Nunn, Allan Ramsay, Alex Wharton, Andy Walter, Christian Wright, Geoff Pesche, Ian Jones, Matthew Cocker, Sean Magee, Simon Gibson, Steve Rooke, Peter Mew*

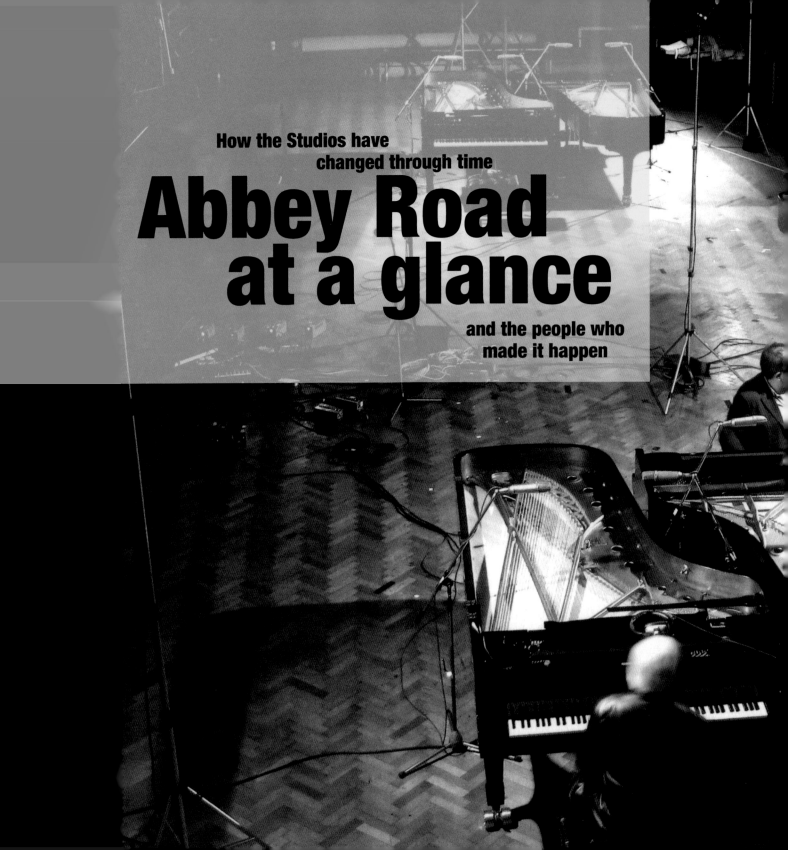

**How the Studios have
changed through time**

Abbey Road
at a glance

**and the people who
made it happen**

Key moments in time:
a brief history

1931 Abbey Road Studios – then known as EMI Studios – opens its doors at 3 Abbey Road, St John's Wood, London, on 12th November. A converted nine-bedroom Georgian house, it took two years to renovate the property into the world's first custom-built recording studio. Prior to the opening of the bespoke studios engineers visited artists in person, or used makeshift facilities at EMI's Maiden Lane base.

*Left: Fred Gaisberg and William Sinkler Darby – EMI recording engineers whose work paved the way for the creation of Abbey Road Right: Catalan-Spanish Pablo Casals – one of the famous classical musicians to record at Abbey Road during the 1930s Below: Stills from the film strip **Nipper Runs Amok**, in which the dog from the iconic HMV logo takes issue with a gramophone*

1931 Distinguished composer Sir Edward Elgar conducts the London Symphony Orchestra in Studio 1 for the Studios' official opening ceremony. Irish playwright Sir George Bernard Shaw, composer Sir Walford Davies, and conductor Sir Landon Ronald attend. Elgar addresses his orchestra: "Good morning gentlemen. A very light programme this morning. Please play as if you've never heard it before."

1931 Pre-eminent audio engineer and prolific inventor Alan Dower Blumlein – based at EMI's Central Research Laboratories – lodges the patent for 'binaural' sound, essential for stereo records, films, and surround sound. He also patents the HB1A microphone. Within a few

months the HB1A was being used extensively by the BBC and Abbey Road. The following year the fifth, and best, version appeared –the HB1E. Their sound quality is famed for its unique character and warmth.

1934 Conductor Thomas Beecham and producer Walter Legge meet and begin their long collaboration.

1937 The coronation of King George VI on 12th May is recorded through a land line from Westminster Abbey, via the BBC, to Abbey Road Studios.

1940 Abbey Road Studios remain open and in use during the war years and are involved in recordings for the British government and radio broadcasts for the BBC. Prime Minister Winston Churchill's broadcasts are simultaneously recorded at Abbey Road and subsequently released by EMI as a set of records bearing his image.

1944 Seminal US big band leader Glenn Miller collaborates with singer Dinah Shore in Studio 1. These were the last recordings made by Miller – a US serviceman in the Second World War – before his death in a plane accident. Incredibly, they remained unreleased for 50 years until his *Lost Recordings* album was finally issued in 1996.

Near right: *Sir Malcolm Sargent, regarded as among the finest choral conductors in the world, at work during the 1960s*
Far right: *Russian conductor Efrem Kurtz – a collaborator with Abbey Road mainstay Yehudi Menuhin – conducts during the 1960s*

1947 EMI's landmark BTR magnetic tape recorder is invented. The technology for the BTR was discovered after a team of engineers, which included Abbey Road Studios' E.W. Berth-Jones, inspected captured German equipment.

1950 George Martin begins work at Abbey Road Studios as assistant to Oscar Preuss, then the head of EMI's Parlophone record label. He would later become EMI's most famous producer.

1952 Max Bygraves' **Cowpuncher's Cantata** becomes the first track recorded at Abbey Road Studios to enter the official UK singles charts.

1953 EMI launches the LA 2A – its first portable tape recorder. This allowed 'field work' to be completed by Abbey Road's Mobile Recording Units with greater ease. The BBC also ordered 50 of the LA 2As.

1954 **Oh Mein Papa** by trumpeter Eddie Calvert charts at No. 1, and earns him the distinction of being the first artist to top the UK Singles Chart with a recording made at Abbey Road Studios.

1957 Cliff Richard auditions at Abbey Road Studios for producer Norrie Paramor. Part of an initiative by EMI and Abbey Road to create home-grown rock 'n' roll, Richard establishes himself as one of the most successful British pop artists of all time.

1961 British pop star Helen Shapiro becomes one of the youngest artists to record at Abbey Road when she auditions, aged 14. In the three years that followed she recorded 11 hit singles.

From left: *Famed Abbey Road producer George Martin works with British entertainer Leslie Phillips during the 1960s; The Neumann U47 microphone – one of the most popular vintage microphones at Abbey Road; British pop star Cliff Richard in his early days, at the Studios*

1962 The most famous pop band of all time – The Beatles – make their first demo at Abbey Road. The session is recorded during the evening of Sunday 6th June, and the Liverpool quartet return three months later as contracted EMI artists. During the session they record their first single – **Love Me Do**.

1962 Sellers and Milligan record **Bridge on the River Wye** parody – one of the most famous comedy albums recorded at Abbey Road.

1964 EMI introduces its REDD.51 recording desks to the Studios – the model famously used to great experimental success by the Beatles.

1966 Abbey Road engineer and eventual head of the Studios, Ken Townsend, invents artificial double-tracking. A time saving innovation that emulated the sound of an artist recording the same part twice – used heavily by The Beatles it led to other effects such as flanging.

1969 The Beatles record their final album – **Abbey Road.** It becomes their most successful release to date, and EMI changes the building's name to Abbey Road Studios in response.

1973 Music pioneers Pink Floyd release their multi-million-selling **Dark Side of the Moon** album, recorded at Abbey Road. Its success ushers in a new breed of popular music recording artist. They replace the clean-cut pop of the 1960s with something less obviously commercial, and predisposed to a large amount of sonic experimentation.

Far left: *A J37, one of the many Studer tape machines at Abbey Road, first introduced during the 1960s*
Left: *EMI director Bob Mercer with recording artists Kate Bush and Steve Harley*
Below: *Nipper continues to cause chaos*

Clockwise, from top left: *Recordings from the EMI Classics label by Barbara Hendricks, Han-Na Chang, John McGinn, Angela Gheorghiu and Roberto Alagna, and Ole Edvard Antonsen. Formed in 1990, the label rejuvenated EMI's classical output.*

Right: *Corinne Bailey Rae performs as part of* **Live From Abbey Road** *– a series of in situ sessions from the Studios first televised in 2006*

Far right: *Former Beach Boys member Brian Wilson on* **Live From Abbey Road**

1980 Abbey Road opens a fourth recording studio: The Penthouse. It is now the only studio at Abbey Road with a digital rather than analogue mixing desk, and originally housed a 48-track mixing desk despite being the smallest of all the studios.

1984 Abbey Road launches its post-production services. The advent of CDs creates demand for remastered EMI back catalogue reissues on the new format.

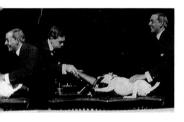

1988 Studio 3 is refurbished to include lounge, kitchen, and bathroom areas – creating a private, self-contained space for artists. The control room is also refitted with two digital multi-track tape machines and the latest Calrec desk. The redesign introduces a room to the rear of Studio 3, the walls of which are lined with non-parallel mirrors.

1997 The Studios' new interactive technology team produces the first commercially available DVD in the UK – Queen's *Greatest Flix*. This is followed by the first feature film on DVD, *The Graduate*.

1999 The development of 5.1 'surround-sound' recording is utilized by Abbey Road engineers for music in addition to film scores with the re-release and remastering of The Beatles' *Yellow Submarine Songtrack*. Ultimately, 5.1 does not replace stereo as the standard audio format, but this remains one of the technology's highest-profile releases.

2001 Big movie franchises *Harry Potter* and *Lord of the Rings* movie series record, mix and master the first instalments of their respective series at the Studios.

2000 Abbey Road's Online Mixing & Mastering website launches, enabling the world to use Studios' expertise and equipment from the comfort of their own homes. The mastering element goes online in 2009, followed by mixing in 2011.

2010 The pedestrian crossing outside the Studios made famous by The Beatles on the front cover of their *Abbey Road* album is awarded Grade II listed status. It continues to attract over 600,000 visitors a year – all keen to recreate the famous photograph.

Who's who?
The Studio's famous faces

Malcolm Addey
Engineer, **British**
An Abbey Road staff member from 1958 to 1968, Addey worked on innumerable recordings during his career at the Studios. He is famous for his innovative 'close mixing' technique, which fast became widespread practice as it greatly increased the volume and clarity of individual instruments.

Sir John Barbirolli
Conductor and cellist, **British**
Initially a cellist in the London Symphony Orchestra, Barbirolli, nicknamed 'Glorious John', became a conductor in the 1920s. He went on to record numerous works in Studio 1 by composers such as Schubert and Brahms.

Lionel Bart
Writer and composer, **British**
The writer of musicals such as *Blitz!* and *Oliver!* during the 1960s, Bart also wrote the music for the play *Fings Ain't Wot They Used T'Be*. The West End cast of the latter recorded its soundtrack at Abbey Road, with Bart involved in the sessions. He returned to the Studios in 1989 to record the advertising jingle *Happy Endings*.

Shirley Bassey
Singer, **British**
The Welsh vocalist is arguably most famous for recording the theme songs for three films in the James Bond franchise: *Goldfinger, Moonraker*, and *Diamonds Are Forever*. Her first recording at Abbey Road was 1959's *The Fabulous Shirley Bassey*.

The Beatles
Musicians, **British**
The most successful pop group of all time. The Beatles became synonymous with Abbey Road when they named an album after the street on which the building formerly known as EMI Recording Studios can be found in north-west London. Their experimentation during their sessions at the Studios changed the course of popular music forever.

Sir Thomas Beecham
Conductor, **British**
The founder of the London Philharmonic and Royal Philharmonic orchestras is widely regarded as one of the greatest conductors of all time. His recordings at Abbey Road were numerous, and typified by his tendency towards unpredictable behaviour – often making changes to pieces at the last minute before recording.

Cilla Black
Singer, **British**
Best-selling female artist of the 1960s, Black was part of the stable of pop acts signed by EMI who recorded at Abbey Road and challenged the dominance of American rock 'n' roll in the UK Singles Chart. She later retired from music and forged a successful career as a television presenter.

Alan Dower Blumlein
Engineer, **British**
A gifted engineer and prolific inventor, Blumlein had 128 patents to his name before his premature death in 1942. His most famous inventions include binaural (or stereo) sound, the Ultra-Linear amplifier, and the H2S radar system., elements of which are still in use today.

Sir Adrian Boult
Conductor, **British**
Boult served as the director of music at the British Broadcasting Corporation, establishing the BBC Symphony Orchestra during his time there, before taking the role of chief conductor at the London Philharmonic Orchestra. He recorded numerous pieces at Abbey Road with several British orchestras.

Peter Bown
Engineer, **British**
One of the first Abbey Road engineers to specialize in pop, Peter Bown also worked with seminal prog-rock artists Pink Floyd. A slight eccentric, he is reported to have painted plastic skin over his fingertips in the control room during one session because he was worried they would wear out.

Kate Bush
Singer/songwriter, **British**
Kate Bush signed to EMI in 1975 and topped the UK Single Chart with her debut single, *Wuthering Heights*, in 1978. In 2002, she received an Ivor Novello Award for Outstanding Contribution to British Music. Bush began her recording career at Abbey Road, and has a fondness for Studio 2.

Maria Callas
Singer, **Greek**
The acclaimed soprano was reputedly not a fan of the Studios, but first recorded at Abbey Road in Studio 1 in 1958. Her career included notable performances of operas and works by Verdi, recorded during the 1958 session at the Studios, along with Puccini, Wagner, and others.

Eddie Calvert
Musician, **British**
Trumpet-player Calvert has the distinction of providing Abbey Road its first No. 1 in the UK Singles Chart with instrumental piece *O Mein Papa* in 1954. Prior to his hit, he had become noted for his virtuoso performances in a number of brass bands.

Pablo Casals
Cellist, **Catalan-Spanish**
A gifted cellist, Casals found international stardom with solo, chamber, and classical performances. Abbey Road was the venue for the recording of his famous *Bach Suites*. He also recorded works by Elgar and Beethoven at the Studios, among others.

Maurice Chevalier
Entertainer, **French**
An actor, singer, and dancer, Chevalier unsurprisingly appeared on screen in a number of musicals. He released several successful songs, such as *Thank Heaven for Little Girls* – recorded at the Studios in 1962 – and the theme for the animated Disney movie *The Aristocats*.

Winston Churchill
Politician, **British**
The wartime prime minister recorded his broadcasts via Abbey Road during the Second World War. One of his visits to the Studios also lives on in infamy after he remarked that the white coats worn by the engineers made him feel as if he were visiting a hospital.

Alma Cogan
Singer, **British**
Cogan's commercial success provided EMI with one of their first victories in the world of home-grown pop music. Her dominance during the 1950s continued into the early part of the 60s – her career overlapping slightly with the new wave of Abbey Road recording artists, such as The Beatles.

William Sinkler Darby
Engineer, **American**
One of the pioneers of recorded music, Darby began his career at Emile Berliner's laboratory before he embarked on extensive international travel alongside Fred Gaisberg. Regarded as a brilliant engineer, his recording techniques laid the groundwork for the technology behind Abbey Road.

Bette Davis
Actress, **American**
Towards the end of a long and distinguished career in Hollywood, Davis made the decision to record a solo album at Abbey Road. Unlike many other actors who recorded at the Studios, she was not noted for her singing voice and the album, *Miss Bette Davis*, remains a remarkable footnote from the maverick performer.

Peter Dawson
Singer, **Australian**
A phenomenally successful baritone, Dawson was one of the Studios' earliest recording artists. His recording career with EMI predates the opening of Abbey Road. One of his earliest hits was his 1917 rendition of *The Cobbler's Song*, recorded after he had scanned the music only once.

Alexandre Desplat
Composer, **French**
The multi-award-winning film composer has worked at Abbey Road on various projects. His work there includes the final two films of the Harry Potter series – *The Deathly Hallows*, the animated version of Roald Dahl's children's classic *Fantastic Mr Fox*, and historical drama *The King's Speech*.

Sir Edward Elgar
Composer, **British**
The seminal composer made many recordings at Abbey Road, and was tasked with conducting an orchestra in Studio 1 during its opening ceremony in 1931 – guiding the London Symphony Orchestra through a rendition of *Land of Hope and Glory*. Elgar was receptive to making recordings of his work at a time when it was uncommon – he is one of the earliest studio recording artists.

Stuart Eltham
Engineer, **British**

Along with Peter Bown, Eltham worked on an increased number of sessions during the 1960s because of his adeptness at balancing pop music. He also worked as a sound effects engineer on early comedy recordings and travelled with the Mobile Unit.

Adam Faith
Entertainer, **British**

A star of TV, film, and music, Faith broke new ground at Abbey Road as an artist recording original material during the 1960s. He also recorded the soundtrack for his film *Beat Girl* at the Studios in 1960. He then retired from music, but came back into the public eye as he continued his acting career across film and TV.

Flanders and Swann
Entertainers, **British**

A comedy duo, Michael Flanders and Donald Swann combined music and humorous anecdotes in the music hall tradition. They recorded two of their comedy revues at Abbey Road during the 1960s, shortly before they dissolved their partnership.

Edward Fowler
Engineer, **British**

Nicknamed 'Chick', Edward Fowler was an experienced audio engineer who was part of both EMI's initial Mobile Recording Unit venture and the management at Abbey Road. He worked for the Studios from 1946 until 1967, when he retired as its General Manager. His recordings with pianist and composer Artur Schnabel in the 1930s are an early example of his famed quality recordings.

Freddie and the Dreamers
Musicians, **British**

Part of the wave of young recording artists that emerged from Abbey Road in the 1960s, diminutive frontman Freddie Garrity and his band began their recording career at Abbey Road. Unlike many of their peers, the group never disbanded and continued to perform until 2000.

Fred Gaisberg
Engineer, **American**

The highest-profile recording engineer from the early days of recorded music, Gaisberg travelled the world on behalf of the Gramophone Company. He hauled the then cutting-edge recording technology across oceans and borders. He documented his adventures in his diaries and letters, which have survived him.

Gerry and the Pacemakers
Musicians, **British**

Another Merseyside act who achieved chart success by recording at Abbey Road during the 1960s, the group's first hit single was their *How Do You Do It?* debut in 1963. Frontman Gerry Marsden collaborated with Beatle Paul McCartney years later in 1989 for a charity record following the Hillsborough football stadium disaster.

Beniamino Gigli
Singer, **Italian**

The world-famous tenor performed regularly, from a series of high-profile debuts in the 1910s to shortly before his death in 1957. He also starred in more than 20 films during this period. His London recordings of operatic pieces took place at Abbey Road.

Michael Gleason and Fraser Kennedy
Producer and Associate Producer, **American and British**

The driving force behind the *Live from Abbey Road* television series, Gleason and Kennedy brought a diverse range of heritage, modern, and new artists through the doors of the Studios to record in an intimate live setting.

The Hollies
Musicians, **British**

One of the 1960s pop acts from the UK to mimic the close-harmony style of American rock 'n' roll from the previous decade, The Hollies were initially a Parlophone act. They recorded at Abbey Road, and have stayed together for over 40 years, continuing to perform today.

Billy J Kramer
Singer, **British**

A Merseybeat artist who recorded at Abbey Road during the 1960s, Kramer shared a producer and manager – George Martin and Brian Epstein – with the Beatles. He split from his backing band, The Dakotas, following the decline of Merseybeat but has recorded as a solo artist.

John Leckie
Producer, **British**

Leckie was a balance engineer at Abbey Road, working with the likes of John Lennon, George Harrison, and Pink Floyd. He left his position in 1978 to become a freelance producer, and has since produced successful albums for British bands such as XTC, The Stone Roses, Radiohead, and Muse.

Walter Legge
Producer, **British**

Founder of the Philharmonia Orchestra and a pre-eminent classical producer, Legge rose to prominence when he began working with Sir Thomas Beecham at Abbey Road in the 1930s. He left EMI after a disagreement, but continued to record his wife – opera singer Elisabeth Schwarzkopf – for them.

Humphrey Lyttelton
Entertainer, **British**

A jazz artist signed to Parlophone during George Martin's tenure as the label's head, Lyttelton's most famous recording was the 1956 single *Bad Penny Blues* which was sampled on The Beatles Lady Madonna. He later pursued a career as a broadcaster, presenting the BBC radio comedy *I'm Sorry I Haven't a Clue.*

Opposite, left: *Glen Miller records at Abbey Road with collaborator Dinah Shore*
Opposite, right: *Yehudi Menuhin signs the labels on one of his early releases for HMV*
From left: *Cliff Richard and The Shadows record during the 1950s ; Matt Monro watches producer George Martin at the control desk during the 1960s*
Below:
Pink Floyd

Sir George Martin
Producer, **British**

The most famous producer in the Studios' history. Martin joined EMI in 1950 as an assistant to Oscar Preuss, and eventually replaced his mentor as head of the Parlophone label. He left that position in 1965 to set up his own studios – AIR – but continued to return to Abbey Road to work with recording artists there.

Giles Martin
Producer, **British**

Also a composer and arranger, Martin co-produced, with his father, the Grammy award-winning soundtrack for **Love**, the Beatles/Cirque du Soleil show. In 2008-2009 he was involved in the development of, and music production for, the hugely successful music video game **The Beatles: Rockband**

Yehudi Menuhin
Violinist, **American**

Born to Russian-Jewish parents in New York City, Menuhin later became a Swiss citizen. He recorded frequently at Abbey Road in his long, distinguished career. A classical virtuoso violinist, he also dabbled in world music latterly. He remained one of the few contracted classical stars at EMI, such was his enduring popularity.

Glenn Miller
Bandleader, **American**

Miller's remarkable compositional skills established him in the USA during the 1940s. Serving in the Second World War, duty brought him to Abbey Road to record. Tragically, it was to be his last session as his plane to France disappeared over the Channel.

Mickie Most
Producer, **British**

Most was one of the more entrepreneurial producers of the golden age of pop music. He mainly produced artists for EMI's Columbia label at Abbey Road, but also set up his own label – RAK – and a recording studio of the same name located not far from Abbey Road near Regents Park, London.

Ruby Murray
Singer, **British**

Belfast-born Ruby Murray first recorded at the Studios during the 1950s as one of EMI's early home-grown pop stars. She toured internationally during the decade, and made numerous appearances on stage and TV. Her heyday was commemorated with a 50th anniversary set of her recordings in 2005.

Norman Newell
Producer, **British**

A former head of EMI's Columbia label, Newell produced and wrote for many pop artists who recorded at Abbey Road – predominantly during the 1950s and 60s. He also made several cast recordings of popular West End musicals – an innovation that later became common practice for such productions. He received several awards for his work and compositions.

James Newton Howard
Composer, **American**

Nominated for eight Academy Awards, Newton Howard is also a songwriter, record producer, conductor, and keyboardist in addition to his work as a composer of film scores. In 2010 he was appointed Visiting Professor of Media Composition at the Royal Academy of Music in London.

Norrie Paramor
Producer, **British**

Paramor was originally signed to EMI as a recording artist, but found fame as a producer for Columbia. His hits included Eddie Calvert's **O Mein Papa** and several Ruby Murray recordings. Paramor wrote many of his own songs and scores and left EMI in 1968 to set up his own company, which released the No. 1 hit **Lily the Pink** by The Scaffold through Parlophone.

Alan Parsons
Producer and musician, **British**

An assistant engineer on The Beatles' **Abbey Road** album, Alan Parsons became synonymous with prog rock after working as an engineer for Pink Floyd. He then formed his supergroup, The Alan Parsons Project, which was also centred around the Studios – with its revolving cast of musicians who worked there in the 70s.

Pink Floyd
Musicians, **British**

Pink Floyd's willingness to improvise and experiment led to seminal albums that ushered in the psychedelic rock movement, altering the pop landscape of the 1970s. The band also embraced the Studios' multi-track recording technology, which had now become standard.

Oscar Preuss
A&R Manager, **British**

The head of EMI's Parlophone label from its formation in 1923 until his retirement in 1950, Oscar Preuss was responsible for shaping much of the musical output at Abbey Road. He often decided which artists should be demo'ed and signed. His vision built one of the most successful labels in the history of recorded music.

Walter Ridley
Producer, **British**
Ridley was hired by EMI to build a pop music roster for its HMV label in 1949, and worked for the company until his retirement in 1977. During that time he discovered numerous successful artists that changed the perception of HMV as a predominantly classical label, also writing over 200 songs of his own.

Paul Robeson
Singer, **American**
Robeson led a varied and eventful life, and was famously blacklisted in 1950 because of his support for the Communist party. Although this impeded his ability to travel and perform, he recorded at Abbey Road before and after this period

of turmoil. He is now remembered for his politics, scholarly pursuits, and artistic endeavours.

Allan Rouse
Engineer, **British**
Abbey Road engineer Allan Rouse formed an integral part of the Beatles remastering project, which was undertaken to embrace new technology and provide definitive mono, stereo, and 5.1 versions of the recordings. Rouse's work was praised by the surviving Beatles for its ambition and technical proficiency.

Sir Malcolm Sargent
Conductor, **British**
A standard-bearer for both choral and orchestral music, Sargent is regarded

by many as the pre-eminent conductor of his day. Sargent recorded at the Studios with the London Symphony Orchestra, among others.

Artur Schnabel
Pianist, **Austrian**
Famed as an exponent of Beethoven's piano music, Schnabel worked with Edward Fowler and Malcolm Sargent at Abbey Road. As his recordings predated magnetic-tape technology, Schnabel's sessions were particularly gruelling – he was required to record epic renditions on wax. He recorded both concertos and sonatas at the Studios.

Dame Elisabeth Schwarzkopf
Singer, **German**
Signed to EMI after the Second

World War by Walter Legge, Elisabeth Schwarzkopf's recordings at Abbey Road were also produced by her eventual husband. The couple married in 1953 and Schwarzkopf continued to perform regularly with opera companies around the world. Following Legge's departure from EMI, she joined him in giving masterclasses.

Ken Scott
Producer, **British**
Scott began his career at Abbey Road working as an engineer for some of its most famous artists, such as The Beatles and Pink Floyd. He left the Studios in the 1970s, and famously went on to produce several of David Bowie's albums from that period – which forged a new genre of high-concept glam rock.

Andrés Segovia
Guitarist, **Spanish**
Early classical recordings at Abbey Road enabled Segovia to re-establish the guitar as a respected instrument for the performance of classical music. He recorded on several occasions at Abbey Road – initially during the 1930s and for the last time in 1949. By this time his modern-romantic style had firmly established itself.

Peter Sellers
Comedian, **British**
Peter Sellers is the biggest international comedy star to have recorded at Abbey Road Studios. Sellers' albums with

George Martin – *The Best of Sellers* in 1958 and *Songs for Swinging Sellers* in 1959 – were part of the producer's programme of work with other comedians such as Spike Milligan, Peter Cook, and Peter Ustinov. The material proved that they could be just as innovative as musicians inside a recording studio.

Helen Shapiro
Singer, **British**
Signed by Norrie Paramor while still in her mid-teens, Shapiro's trademark husky voice set her apart from other female recording artists of her day. Her recording career flourished during the 1950s and 1960s. She subsequently transitioned to acting, but continued to perform on occasion and notably collaborated with Humphrey Lyttleton during the 1980s.

Norman 'Hurricane' Smith
Producer, **British**
The producer of three Pink Floyd albums, Smith frequently clashed with the group over their differing approaches to recording music. He had previously worked as an engineer for The Beatles, among others, and his unlikely hit solo single, 1971's *Don't Let It Lie*, was originally composed for John Lennon.

Marc Streitenfeld
Composer, **German**
Starting out as a music editor and supervisor, Streitenfeld is now known for his collaborations with director

Ridley Scott. The scores for **Robin Hood** (2010) and **Prometheus** (2012) were produced at Abbey Road Studios with engineer Peter Cobbin.

Ken Townsend
Engineer, **British**
Townsend was the inventor of automatic double-tracking and former engineer for the Beatles. He was also Abbey Road's longest-serving director. Now retired, Townsend's other notable achievements include the design of the Penthouse Studio, renovation of the Studios' building, and the partnership with Anvil Films – which introduced regular film score work to Studio 1, saving it from being spilt into smaller units.

Vanessa-Mae
Musician, **British**
A self-styled fusion violinist, Vanessa-Mae was born in Singapore, raised in Britain, and is of part-Thai descent. She began her musical career as a child, but later signed for EMI and recorded at Abbey Road. Her multi-platinum album **The Violin Player** was partly recorded at the Studios in 1995.

John Williams
Composer, **American**
The most successful film score composer in the history of cinema first recorded at Abbey Road during the early 1980s as part of his work on the **Star Wars** franchise. Williams' other famous scores include **Jaws**, **Indiana**

Jones, **Superman**, and **Jurassic Park**. He also scored three films in the **Harry Potter** series at the Studios.

Eric Woolfson
Musician, **British**
The co-founder of the Alan Parsons Project, Woolfson had previously worked as a songwriter for other artists. He later transitioned into writing musicals. His fourth, **Poe** – based on the life and works of Edgar Allan Poe – was the first production of its type to be staged at the Studios. It premiered in Studio 1 in 2003.

Hazel Yarwood
Engineer, **British**
A highly skilled veteran of Abbey Road's cutting room, Yarwood was one of the first women to hold a technical job at the Studios. Her expertise at cutting, in both classical and pop, has resulted in her work being well-regarded by audiophiles and fans for its clarity and fidelity.

Gabriel Yared
Composer, **Lebanese**
Best known for his collaborations with the late British director Anthony Minghella, Yared has been composing original scores for films since 1980. The soundtracks for both **The Talented Mr. Ripley** (1999) and **Cold Mountain** (2003) were recorded at Abbey Road.

Opposite, from left: *Helen Shapiro and Norrie Paramor work together in Studio 2; Artur Schnabel (left) consults Sir Adrian Boult*
Left: *Elisabeth Schwarzkopf poses for a publicity shot*
Right: *Sir Henry Wood with conductor's baton in hand*
Above: *Vanessa-Mae performs 'techno-fusion' on a trademark electric violin*

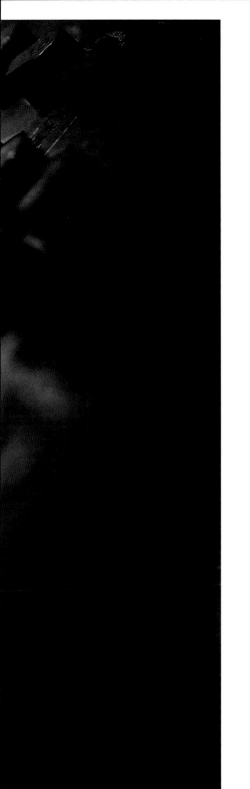

Afterword

When we first discussed producing a book to celebrate our history we were faced with a difficult reality. What should we include and what do we exclude? Our story is packed full of defining moments. Our rooms have hosted some of the finest recordings ever made, great artists, composers and musicians, not to mention producers, engineers and technicians who are at the heart of our piece of the creative process. A comprehensive history is an immense undertaking that would take many more pages and years to compile. We hope to take on that challenge one day but time lines and operating constraints call for the production of a more concise version this time.

The Abbey Road Studios story is a fabulous one and this book is a wonderful chronicle. We are all proud of it. We believe we truly are the best studio in the world but consider ourselves fortunate to have so much talent come through our doors to make music every day. Everyone at Abbey Road extends their thanks and appreciation to all those who continue to patronise the Studios. A great studio is nothing without great music. Our only regret is that we did not have the space to mention so many of you.

Jonathan Smith
Senior Vice President, EMI Studios

"One can sense the presence of the great engineers and producers of the past, long since gone.

Names which may mean little to the average man, but great people such as Arthur Clarke, Dougie Larter, Bob Beckett, Charlie Anderson, Walter Legge, Charlie Thomas, and my own dear mentor, Oscar Preuss, who taught me so much. These men flew the record industry in open cockpits by the seat of their pants, and paved the way for the modern, jetstream, computerized machine that today's young talents have to guide."

Sir George Martin, *Abbey Road*

Index

Acknowledgements

Bloomsbury Publishing would like to thank the many Abbey Road staff, past and present, who helped us with this book.

Special thanks to Kate Calloway, Gary Pietronave and Chris Jones, photographic archivists at EMI Archives UK & Ireland, for selecting, digitising and researching the wonderful stories behind the majority of the book's images – It is due to their experience, knowledge and hard work that this book has been possible. And to Wayne Shevlin – Director, EMI Archives UK & Ireland and Abbey Road Studios Business Systems – for project management and coordination. Also thanks to Sonita Cox, archivist, and Jackie Bishop, EMI Archives manager, for their assistance with research and access to EMI's archive collection.

Photos pre-1946 are provided courtesy of the EMI Group Archive Trust, a charitable organisation which preserves the early heritage of The Gramophone Company and EMI. Thanks to Joanna Hughes, the Trust's Heritage Curator, for her help. Little Nipper is reproduced with the permission of HMV.

Many thanks to Abbey Road's engineers, technical services team, library and staff who contributed much time and effort in research, consultancy, and fact checking: Cary Anning, Colette Barber, Chris Buchanan, Simon Campbell, Peter Cobbin, Jon Eades, Dave Forty, Simon Gibson, Richard Hale, Ian Jones, Jim Jones, Peach Kazen, Lucy Launder, John Leckie, Sean Magee, Peter Mew, Ian Pickavance, Allan Ramsay, Steve Rook, Allan Rouse, Lester Smith, Mirek Stiles, Ken Townsend, Malcolm Walker, and Andrew Walter.

Thanks also to Paul Broucek, Gennaro Castaldo, Tim Chapman, Guy Hayden, Amy Gibson, Michael Gleason, Brian Kehew, Fraser Kennedy, Chris Kuser, Ny Lee, Paul McCarthy, Kerin McDonald, John Otway, Sunny Park, Holly Pearson, Kevin Ryan, Jonathan Smith, Hannah van den Brul, Malcolm Walker, and the Woolfson family for their help and support.

EMI staff photographers: John Dove, Steve Hickey, Ken Palmer, Peter Vernon and A.C.K. Ware.
Other photographers: Bruce Flemming, Jeremy Grayson, Richi Howell and Angus McBean.

The publisher would like to thank the following for their kind permission to reproduce their photographs:
Athena Anastasiou: 238 bottom right, 239 bottom left, bottom centre, bottom right, Tom Bunning: 204 centre, 207 top left, Alexis Chabala: 238 bottom left, Dave Clark: 168 left, 169 right, Peter Cobbin: 4-5, 6-7, 42 top left, centre left, 43, 87, 146-147, 218 centre left, bottom left, 219, 220-221, 222-223, 228-229, 256-257, 286-287, 298-299, Phil Dent: 186, 187 top left, centre left, bottom left, 221top left, centre left, Dreamworks Animation: 218 bottom right, Benjamin Ealovega: 212, 213, 214 top left, top right, 215 top, bottom, right, 216, 217 left, 218 top left, Brian Gibson: 282 left, Billy Green: 221 top right, Richard Hale: 236 top left, centre left; 243, Michael Humphrey: 176-7, Live from Abbey Road: 200-201, 202 top left, centre left, bottom left, 203, 205 left, centre, right, 206, 207 top, bottom, 208, 209, 210 top left, top right, bottom, 211top, bottom, 226 top left, David Nutter: 138-139, Lester Smith: 284 top right

Alamy: front cover; Getty Images: 62 top left (Erich Auerbach), 62 bottom left, 63 top right, 95 (David Farrell), 176 (Matthew Lloyd), 184 (Eduardo Parra), 193 (Paul Bergen), 194 & 195 (Kevin Cummins), 196 (Bernd Muller/Redferns), 197 left (Mick Hutson/Redferns), 197 centre (Diana Scrimgeour/Redferns), 203 inset (RAFA RIVAS/AFP), 204 top left (Fabrice Coffrini/AFP), 204 bottom left. Kobal Collection: 178 (20th Century Fox), 179 (LucasFilm Ltd/Paramount), 180 top (Universal/Embassy), 180 bottom right (Yanco/Tao/Recorded Picture Co.), 181 (Merchant Ivory/Goldcrest), 187 (Icon/Ladd Co./Paramount). Lebrecht: 89, 92 & 93 (Godfrey MacDomnic), 181 bottom right (Paul Tomlins). Rex Features: 94 (Reg Wilson), 168 (Philip Dunn), 170 top left (Andre Csillag), 170 top right (Brian Rasic), 170 bottom (ITV), 196 (Brian Rasic), 197 right (Andre Csillag), 214 bottom left (Moviestore Collection), 217 top left & centre (c. New Line/Everett). Ronald Grant Archive: 180 bottom left, 188, 189. TopFoto: 185.

Every effort has been made to contact all copyright holders of material reproduced in this book. If any have been inadvertently overlooked, the publishers will be pleased to insert the appropriate acknowledgement in any subsequent printing of this publication.